SOLIDWORKS 2019
Design Fundamentals

1st Edition

Jaecheol Koh
ONSIA Inc.

ONSIA

SOLIDWORKS 2019
Design Fundamentals

ISBN: 9781679285714
Independently Published

Author: Jaecheol Koh
Publisher: ONSIA Inc. (www.e-onsia.com)
E-Mail: jckoh@e-onsia.com
Cover Image: Freepik.com

Download Files for Exercises

Visit our homepage www.e-onsia.com. You can download the files for exercises without any limit. This textbook is written in SOLIDWORKS 2019 and the files are available in SOLID-WORKS 2018. Users of earlier releases can use this textbook with minor modifications.

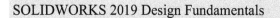
Download Files for Exercises

Visit our homepage www.e-onsia.com. You can download the files for exercises without any limit. This textbook is written in SOLIDWORKS 2019 and the files are available in SOLID-WORKS 2018. Users of earlier releases can use this textbook with minor modifications.

Preface

This textbook explains how to create models with freeform surfaces using SOLIDWORKS 2019. SOLIDWORKS is a three dimensional CAD/CAM/CAE software developed by Dassault Systèms, France. This textbook is based on SOLIDWORKS 2019. Users of earlier releases can use this book with minor modifications. We provide files for exercises via our website. All files are in SOLIDWORKS 2018, so readers can open the files using later releases of SOLIDWORKS.

It is assumed that readers of this textbook have no prior experience in using SOLIDWORKS for modeling 3D parts. This textbook is suitable for anyone interested in learning 3D modeling using SOLIDWORKS.

Each chapter deals with the major functions of creating 3D features using simple examples and step by step self-paced exercises. Additional drawings of 3D parts are provided at the end of each chapter for further self exercises. The final exercises are expected to be completed by readers who have fully understood the content and completed the exercises in each chapter.

Topics covered in this textbook
- Chapter 1: Starting Solidworks
- Chapter 2 and 3: Creating Extruded Feature, Hole, Boolean Operation
- Chapter 4: Understanding Reference Geometries
- Chapter 5: Detailing
- Chapter 6: Parametric Editing
- Chapter 7: Copying Objects
- Chapter 8: Sweep and Loft
- Chapter 9 and 10: Assembly Design
- Chapter 11: Drawing

This page left blank intentionally.

Table of Contents

Chapter 4
Reference Geometries 75

Chapter 5
Detailing 97

Chapter 6
Parametric Editing. 123

Chapter 7
Copy of Objects and Features 145

Chapter 8
Sweep and Loft **163**

Chapter 9
Assembly Design I (Bottom-Up Assembly). **181**

Chapter 10
Assembly Design II (Top-Down Assembly). 199

Chapter 11
Drawing 223

Chapter 1
Starting Solidworks

■ **After completing this chapter you will understand**

- the components and basic operations in Solid-works.

- the basic options of Solidworks.

- the modeling process of Solidworks.

1.1 Introduction to Solidworks

Solidworks is a CAD/CAM/CAE software developed by Dassault System, France. In the CAD category, you can create 3D models, assemblies and drawings. In the CAM category, you can create data for manufacturing. And in the CAE category, you can analyze the engineering problems by using the computer. In this textbook, we will learn how to create 3D models, assemblies, and drawings of a part or an assembly.

1.2 Executing Solidworks

By executing Solidworks, the Solidworks window is invoked as shown in Fig 1-1. You can open the documents for self-paced learning, create a new document and open an existing part documents.

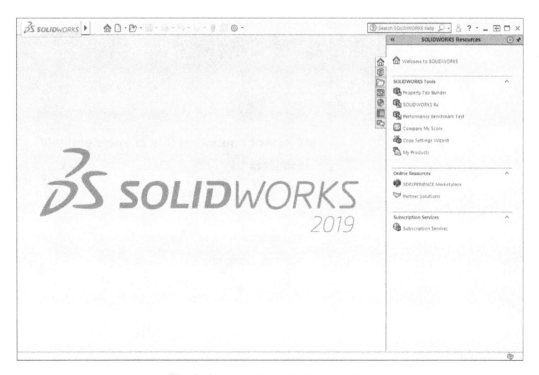

Fig 1-1 Screen Shot of Solidworks 2019

1.3 Creating a New Part Document

By clicking the **Welcome to Solidworks** button(⌂), the **Welcome - Solidworks** dialog box as shown in Fig 1-2 is invoked. If you press the **New > Part** button, the new part window is invoked as shown in Fig 1-3

Fig 1-2 Welcome SOLIDWORKS Dialog Box

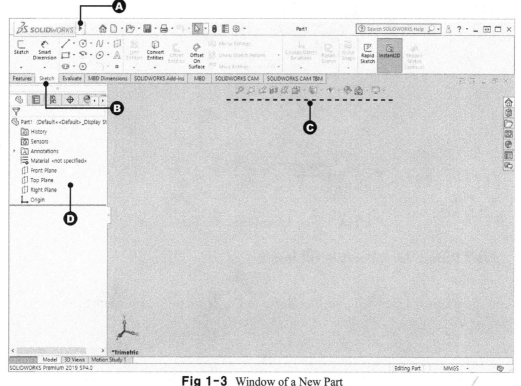

Fig 1-3 Window of a New Part

1.3.1 Menus (🅐 in Fig 1-3)

You can access the menus such as File, Edit, View, Insert, Tools, Window, Help by hovering the mouse pointer on the SOLIDWORKS logo. You can use the icons such as New, Open, Save, etc. when the Solidworks menus are collapsed. You can pin the Solidworks menu by pressing the pin icon at the end of the menu.

1.3.2 Command Manager (🅑 in Fig 1-3)

You can use the Solidworks commands by pressing the corresponding tabs in the Command Manager. In the Features tab, the icons such as Extruded Boss/Base, Revolved Boss/Base, etc. are available. By using the icons in the Sketch tab, you can create curves. By right-clicking on the tab title, you can use the pop-up menu as shown in Fig 1-4 and you can add the command managers such as Surfaces, Sheet Metal, etc.

Fig 1-4 Pop-Up Menu of the Command Manager

1.3.3 Quick View Toolbar (🅒 in Fig 1-3)

You can access the view tools such as Zoom to Fit, Zoom to Area, etc., on the head-up of the graphics window.

1.3.4 Feature Manager Design Tree (❶ in Fig 1-3)

The modeling history is registered in the Feature Manager Design Tree. You can create the first sketch on the Front, Top or Right plane.

1.3.5 Property Manager

The prompt message or the options for a command is displayed in the Property Manager.

Fig 1-5 Property Manager

1.4 Options

You can access the System Options and Document Properties by clicking the Options icon on the right end of the Solidworks menu. The System Options are applied for the current Solidworks session, and the Document Properties are applied for the current docment. You should confirm the dimensions system after creating a new document on the right bottom of the graphics window. You can modify the dimensions system by clicking it as designated in Fig 1-8.

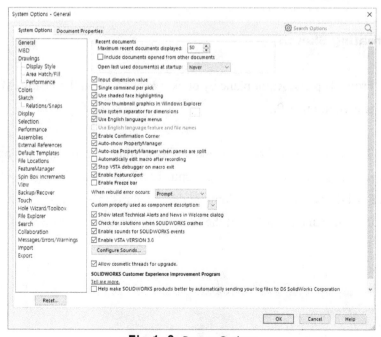

Fig 1-6 System Options

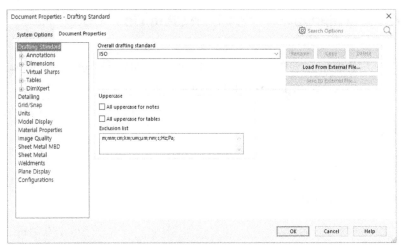

Fig 1-7 Document Properties

Click to Modify

Fig 1-8 Dimension Systems Setting

1.5 Creating Sketch and 3D Model

1.5.1 Creating Sketch

1. Show the Front, Top and Right plane by clicking each one on the FeatureManager Design Tree as shown in Fig 1-9.

2. Select the Front plane and choose the Sketch icon in the pop-up menu. You can right-click on the item to access the full pop-up menu. The Front plane is aligned to the screen as shown in Fig 1-10 and the Sketch Command Manager is invoked. The Exit Sketch icon is activated and you can click it to exit the sketch eivnronment after creating a sketch.

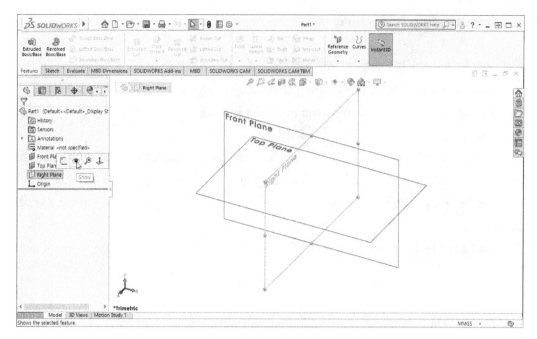

Fig 1-9 Showing Planes

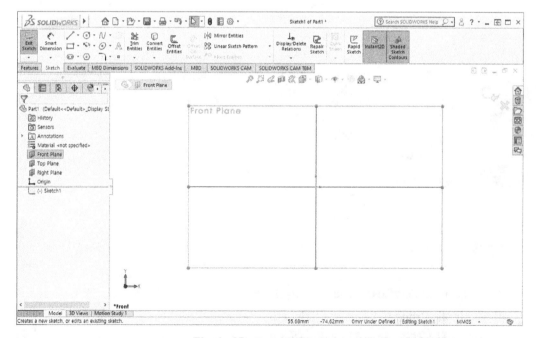

Fig 1-10 Sketch Enviromnent

1.5.2 Creating Rectangle

1. Click the Corner Rectangle icon and click the 1st and 2nd location as shown in Fig 1-11 to create a rectangle. Finish the rectangle by pressing the green checkmark in the FeatureManager Design Tree. You can press the ESC key to finish the Corner Rectangle command.

2. Click the Exit Sketch icon in the Command Manager. Note that the sketch is selected. You can deselect it by clicking the empty area in the graphics window. The rectangle is displayed in grey. You can see that the sketch curves are displayed in blue in the Sketch environment.

3. Press Ctrl+7 to display the Isometric View as shown in Fig 1-12. The planes are hidden.

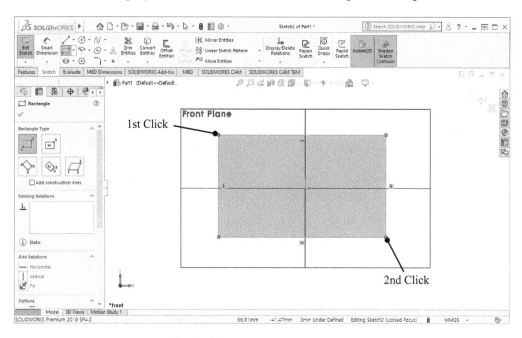

Fig 1-11 Creating Corner Rectangle

1.5.3 Extruding

1. Press the Extruded/Boss Base icon in the Feature command manager. A message is displayed in the Property Manager. Select the rectangle sketch.

2. Drag the head of the arrow to determine the depth of the extrusion.

3. Press the OK button in the Property Manager. The hexadedron is created as shown in Fig 1-14.

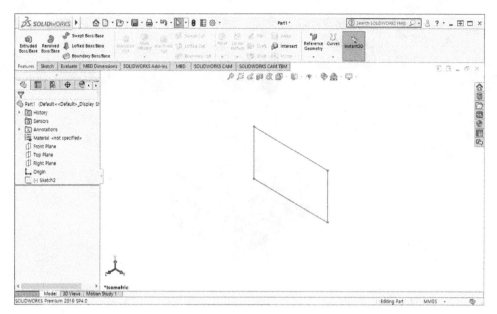

Fig 1-12 Exit Sketch

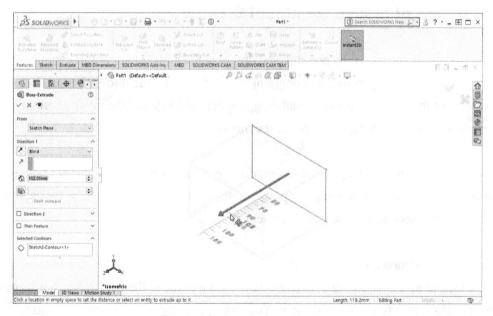

Fig 1-13 Dragging Extrude Depth

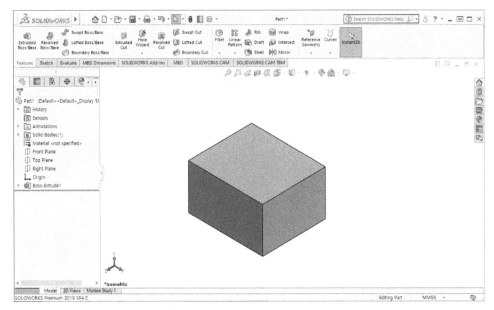

Fig 1-14 Hexahedron Created

1.6 Usage of Mouse for Model Display

You can modify the model by pressing and dragging the middle button of the mouse. You can pan the model by pressing and dragging the Ctrl key and the middle button. You can zoom in/out the model by pressing and dragging the Shift key and the middle button. You can zoom in/out by rolling the wheel of the mouse.

You can fit the model to the graphics window by double clicking the middle button of the mouse. You can fit the model by pressing the corresponding icon in the Quick View toolbar or by pressing the F key as a shortcut.

The view orientation options are available by pressing the Orientation button in the Quick View toolbar as shown in Fig 1-15. You can select a plane in the orientation box around the model to display the normal view. You can access the view orientation options by pressing the Spacebar.

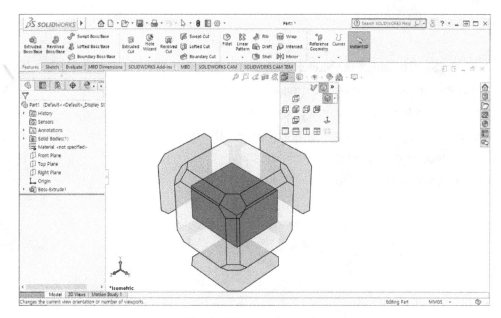

Fig 1-15 View Orientation

1.7 Display Style

You can change the display style of the model by pressing the corresponding button in the Quick View toolbar.

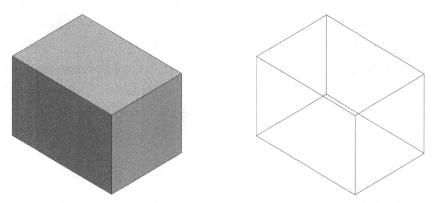

Fig 1-16 Display Style

1.8 Adding

1. Press the Sketch icon in the Sketch command manager.

2. Select the top face of the hexahedron.

3. Press Ctrl + 8 to align the sketch plane to the screen.

4. Create a circle as shownn in Fig 1-17 and exit the sketch. Click the empty area of the graphics window to deselect the sketch.

5. Press Ctrl + 7 to display the isometric view.

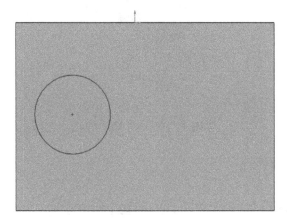

Fig 1-17 Circle

6. Press the Extruded Boss/Base icon in the Feature command manager, select the circle, drag the arrow to determine the depth, and choose the Merge Result option in the property manager. Press the green checkmark on the right corner of the graphics window to add a cylinder to the existing model. You can press the x mark to cancel the command. Select the empty area to deselect the Boss-Extrude feature.

1.9 Removing

1. Select the side face and choose the Sketch icon in the pop-up menu as shown in Fig 1-19.

2. Create the circle and exit the sketch.

3. Press the Extruded Cut icon in the Feature command manager.

4. Drag the arrow as shown in Fig 1-20.

5. Press OK to create a cut feature as shown in Fig 1-21.

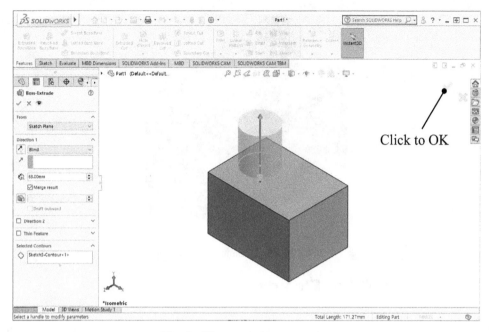

Fig 1-18 Creating Extruded Boss

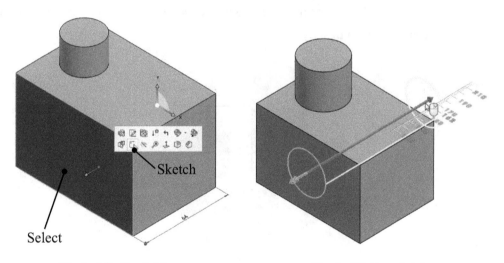

Fig 1-19 Sketch Menu

Fig 1-20 Extruded Cut

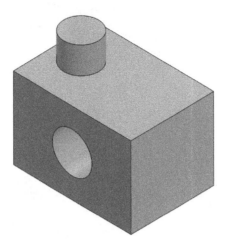

Fig 1-21 Completed Model

1.10 Selecting Other Element

There are restrictions in selecting 3D elements in the 2D screen because there is more than one element under the mouse pointer. In this case, right-click on the desired element and choose Select Other in the pop-up menu. The Select Other window is invoked and you can choose the desired element exactly.

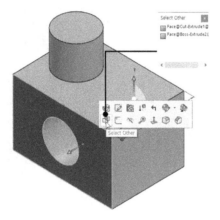

Fig 1-22 Selecting Other Element

1.11 Keyboard Shortcuts

You can customize toolbars or command icons by choosing Tools > Customize in the Solidworks menu. You can set keyboard shortcuts by pressing the Keyboard tab as shown in Fig 1-23.

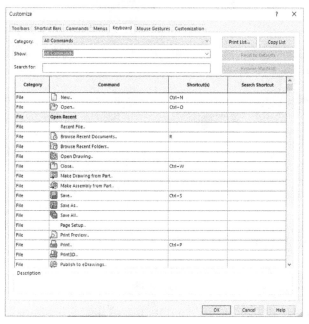

Fig 1-23 Keyboard Shortcut

1.12 Mouse Gesture

Place the mouse pointer on an empty area in the graphics window, right-click and move the mouse a little bit, then the mouse gesture is displayed. You can execute the command rapidly by right-click and dragging the mouse to the corresponding direction. You can set 8 gestures in the Mouse Gestures tab in the Customize dialog box as shown in Fig 1-25

Fig 1-24 Mouse Gestures

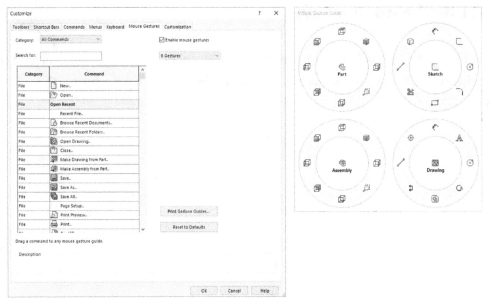

Fig 1-25 Setting Mouse Gestures

1.13 Modifying Template

You can define the properties of a document in the corresponding template file. For example, if you create a new part file, the properties of the part template are applied. As the dimensioning system is pre-defined in the template file, it is required to modify the template file when you are using the inch-pound dimensioning system. You can change the template file according to the following process.

1. Create a new part file.
2. Modify the document properties in Options > Documents Properties.
3. Choose File > Save As in the Solidworks menu.
4. Select the folder "C:\ProgramData\SOLIDWORKS\SOLIDWORKS 2019\templates", choose the Save as Type and overwrite the existing template file Part.prtdot. Note that the folder "ProgramData" is hidden by default. You can show hidden files, folders and drivers by accessing the file explorer options in Windows 10 as shown in Fig 1-27.

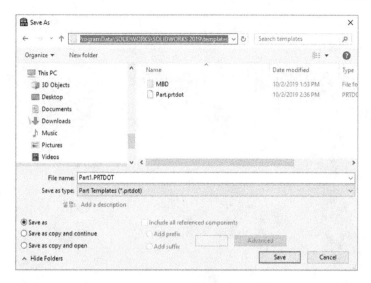

Fig 1-26 Part Template File

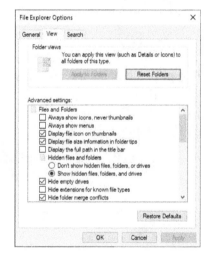

Fig 1-27 Showing Hidden Folder

This page left blank intentionally.

Chapter 2
Sketch and Extrude Basics

■ After completing this chapter you will understand

- how to create and modify the sketch curves.

- how to fully define the sketch curves.

- how to define the contours of an extrusion.

2.1 What is a Sketch?

When you are adding or removing a solid body by using the Extrude or Revolve command, you need a contour defined by a sketch. A solid body is a geometry enclosed by faces and filled with material. Sketch is an wireframe which is defined by curves.

The solid body shown in Fig 2-2 can be created by extruding the closed contour shown in Fig 2-1.

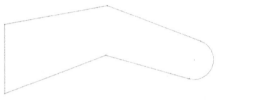

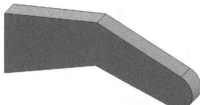

Fig 2-1 Sketch   **Fig 2-2** Extruded Feature

2.2 Sketch Procedure and Components

Let's learn about the general procedure of creating a sketch.

2.2.1 Defining the Sketch Plane

You can define a sketch on a plane. You can use the front, top or right plane as the sketch plane, which is given in the part template. You can also choose a planar face of a solid body as the sketch plane. If you define a sketch plane, the horizontal and vertical axis is defined.

2.2.2 Creating Sketch Curves

After defining the sketch plane, you can create sketch curves by using the commands given in the Sketch tab. At this stage, you can create the curves roughly, but the size and shape of the sketch should be as similar as possible to the desired outcome.

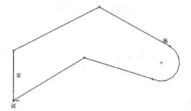

Fig 2-3 Roughly Created Sketch

2.2.3 Constraints

You can define the sketch curves exactly as you want by applying dimensions and adding relations. This process is called a constraining. There are two types of constraints: dimensional constraint and geometrical constraint.

With the dimensional constraint, you use numerical values to define the distance, length, radius, diameter, angle, etc. With the geometrical constraint, you define the shape of a curve by defining its relations with other sketch objects such as horizontal, vertical, coincidence, midpoint, concentric, collinear, equal, etc. The relations are used to define the shape of curves without entering a value. If a curve is fully defined, it turns to black and the status of constraint is displayed at the lower part of the graphics window as shown in Fig 2-4.

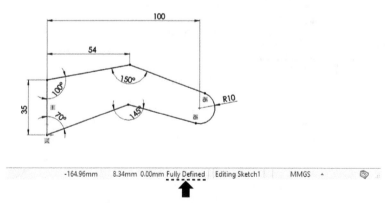

Fig 2-4 Fully Defined Sketch

2.2.4 Exit Sketch

Finish the sketch by clicking the Exit Sketch icon.

2.3 Creating a Line and Constraining

You can create a line or the connected lines and arcs by using the Line command.

2.3.1 Creating a Line

You can create a line by clicking the Line icon and left click-dragging. If you click two locations, you can create the connected lines. Press the ESC key to stop creating connected lines.

The existing relations for the selected lines can be identified in the property manager. You can apply the relations between lines and turn the selected lines into the construction lines or the lines with infinite length.

The under-defined lines are displayed in blue. You can select and drag the under-constrained lines.

To deselect the lines, click an empty area of the graphics window. The Line property manager is invoked by selecting a line.

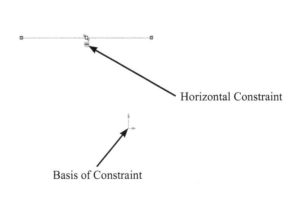

Horizontal Constraint

Basis of Constraint

Fig 2-5 Creating a Line

2.3.2 Fully Defining a Line

The line in Fig 2-5 is applied with the horizontal constraint. The length is not defined, and the relations with the basis of constraint are not defined either. Therefore, you can select the line and drag to move to another location.

You can fully define the line according to the following process.

1. Create a horizontal line.
2. Show the right plane.
3. Press the CTRL key and select both the right plane and the left endpoint of the line.
4. Select Make Coincident in the pop-up toolbar.
5. Press the ESC key.

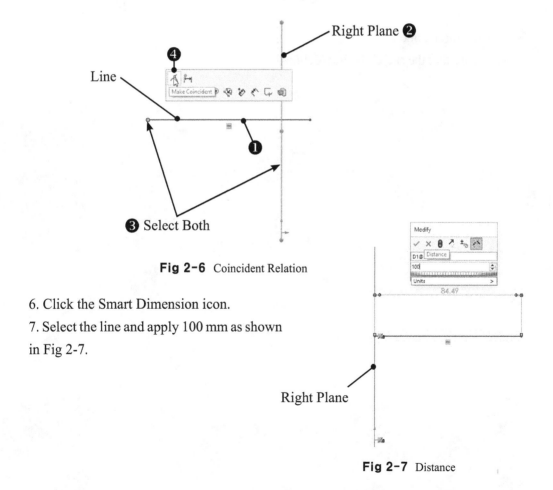

Fig 2-6 Coincident Relation

6. Click the Smart Dimension icon.
7. Select the line and apply 100 mm as shown in Fig 2-7.

Fig 2-7 Distance

8. Apply 50mm distance between the line and the origin.

9. Click an empty area of the graphics window to deselect objects.

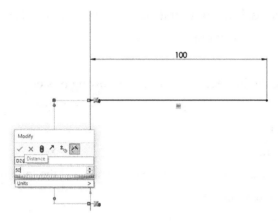

Fig 2-8 Distance

10. Hide the right plane.

11. Make sure that the sketch is fully defined.

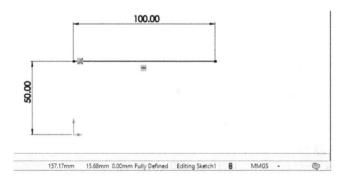

Fig 2-9 Fully Defined

Modify the sketch shown in Fig 2-9 as shown in Fig 2-10. You are expected not to delete the existing line and create a new one, but delete or apply new constraints.

Hints

1. Delete the horizontal constraint and slant the line appropriately by dragging the right endpoint.

2. You can apply the 30° angluar dimension by showing the top plane or by clicking the origin.

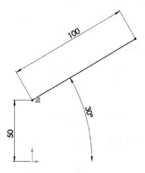

Fig 2-10 Modified Sketch

END of Exercise

2.4 Construction Geometry and Driven Dimension

2.4.1 Construction Geometry

You need a line to apply an angular dimension to constrain the center point of a circle as shown in Fig 2-11. You can change a sketch curve into a construction geometry by right-clicking and choosing the menu. You cannot use the construction geometry to create 3D geometry.

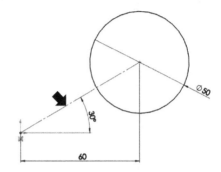

Fig 2-11 Construction Geometry

2.4.2 Driven and Driving Dimension

The sketch shown in Fig 2-11 is fully defined. If you apply a vertical dimension, an option is invoked, as shown in Fig 2-12. You can create it as a driven or a driving dimension.

You cannot modify a driven dimension independently. The vertical dimension in Fig 2-12 is determined by the two existing dimensions 60 mm and 30°. The dimension to drive the sketch curves is called a driving dimension.

If you apply a driving dimension over a fully defined sketch, it turns to over defined. If you double click the status message as shown in Fig 2-13, the SketchXpert is invoked, and you can resolve the over defined status by pressing the Diagnosis or the Manual Repair button.

If you right-click on the over defined dimension, you can turn it into a driven dimension by choosing the option as shown in Fig 2-14 and vice versa.

The driven dimension is not required to define a sketch fully but is applied only for reference.

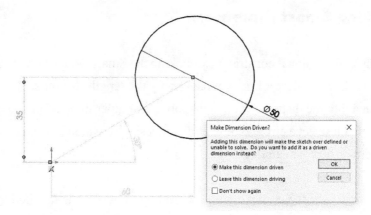

Fig 2-12 Driven or Driving Option

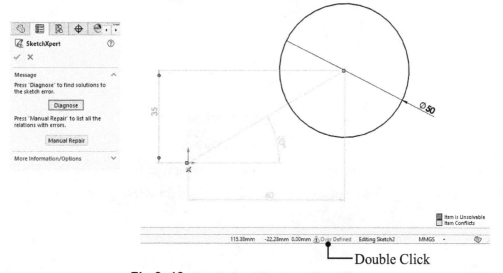

Double Click

Fig 2-13 Over Defined Sketch and SketchXpert

Fig 2-14 Pop-up Menu

2.5 Applying Smart Dimension

You can apply a dimensional constraint by clicking the Smart Dimension icon and selecting the objects. If you select a line, you can apply the length. If you select two parallel lines, you can apply the distance. You can apply the angular dimension by selecting two angled lines. If you select a circle, a diametral dimension is available. And if you select an arc, a radial dimension is available.

If you select a curve without clicking an icon, a pop-up toolbar is invoked, and you can apply the smart dimension. Fig 2-15 shows a pop-up toolbar that is available by selecting a circle.

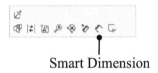

Smart Dimension

Fig 2-15 Pop-up Toolbar

When you are applying a smart dimension, the dimension type is determined by the location of the mouse pointer. You can lock or unlock it by right-clicking the mouse.

Fig 2-16 Types of Dimetrial Dimension

You can recall the Dimension property manager by selecting the dimension line. In the Value tab, you can apply tolerance/Precision or special characters. In the Leader tab, you can modify the types of Witness/Leader display. You can turn the diametral dimension into a radial dimension and vice versa.

Fig 2-17 Dimension Property Manager

2.6 Applying Relations

Click the Add Relation icon and select the objects. The property manager is invoked and you can apply the required relations in the property manager.

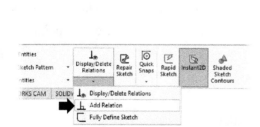

Fig 2-18 Add Relation Icon

Fig 2-19 Property Manager

If you select curves to apply relations, you can apply relations in the Properties property manager as shown in Fig 2-20. You can apply relations in the pop-up toolbar as shown in Fig 2-21. The pop-up toolbar disappears if you move the mouse pointer away from the selections. The toolbar appears if you move the mouse pointer on the selections and pressing the Ctrl key.

Fig 2-20 Properties Property Manager   **Fig 2-21** Pop-up Toolbar

2.7 Type of Relations

The applicable type of relations is determined by the type of selected objects.

Point vs. Point

You can apply the Horizontal, Vertical and Merge relations. By the Horizontal relation, you can make the selected points be aligned horizontally. By the Vertical relation, you can make the selected points be aligned vertically. Here, the points include the endpoint of a curve, the mid-point of a line, the definition points of a spline, the center point of a circle, etc.

Point vs. Line

You can apply the Midpoint and Coincident relations.

Point vs. Circle or Arc

You can apply the Concentric and Coincident relations. Note that you can apply the Midpoint relation between a point and an arc. The Concentric relation constrains a point at the center of a circle or an arc.

Line vs. Line

You can apply the relations such as Horizontal, Vertical, Collinear, Perpendicular, Parallel, etc. The Equal relation makes the selected lines have the same length.

Line vs. Circle or Arc

You can apply the Tangent and Equal Curve Length relations.

Arc vs. Arc

You can apply the Coradial, Tangent, Concentric, Equal, Equal Curve Length relations.

2.8 Snap Options

The snap options are set as shown in Fig 2-23. If you activate the snap options, the corresponding relations are applied while you are creating sketch curves. Fig 2-22 shows the process of creating the second line by snapping to the midpoint of the first line. The midpoint relation is created automatically by choosing the Automatic relations option.

You can deactivate all the snap options by pressing the Ctrl key while you are creating the sketch curves.

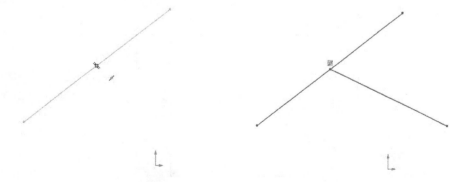

Fig 2-22 Midpoint Relation

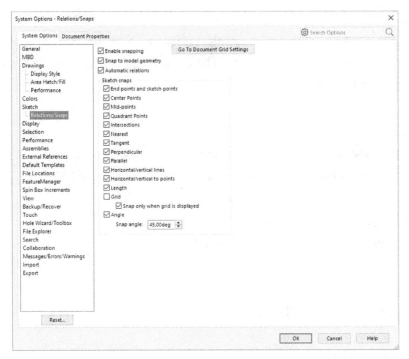

Fig 2-23 Relations/Snaps Settings

Exercise 02   **Fully Defining a Sketch**

Create a sketch on the front plane, fully define it, and extrude by 10 mm. Note that you do not need to apply the same relations shown in the figure.

1. A square of 100 mm length. The origin of the sketch is at the center of the square.

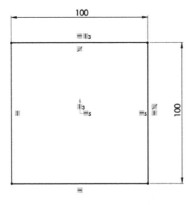

Fig 2-24 Square

2. An equilateral triangle of 100 mm length. The origin of the sketch is at the center of the baseline.

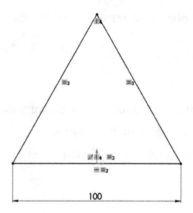

Fig 2-25 Equilateral Triangle

END of Exercise

2.9 Creating Line and Arc

You can create an arc at the end of a line by using the Line command. Create a line and move the mouse cursor to the endpoint of the line. Then move away from the point to your desired direction. If you want to create a line instead of an arc, right-click and choose Switch to Line in the pop-up menu.

Fig 2-26 Creating an Arc Continuously

2.10 Editing Sketch

If you select a sketch in the FeatureManager design tree, the sketch dimensions become visible, and you can modify them by clicking one by one. If you want to modify relations or curves, select the sketch feature and choose Edit Sketch in the pop-up menu.

Exercise 03   Fully Defining a Sketch

Create a sketch on the front plane and extrude it by 10 mm.

Conditions

1. Create the lines and an arc continuously by clicking the Line command.
2. The two lines and an arc are tangent each other.
3. The sharp point is at the origin of the sketch.

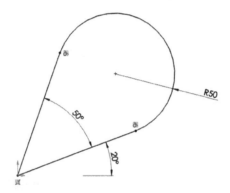

Fig 2-27   Sketch for Exercise 03

END of Exercise

Dimensioning a Circle

You can apply the nearest or the farthest distance by pressing the Shift key while creating a Smart Dimension.

Fig 2-28   Dimensioning a Circle

Create an ellipse, centerpoint arc slot, equilateral hexagon, and fully define them.

1. Create an ellipse on the front plane. The major axis is slanted by 20° about the Top plane.

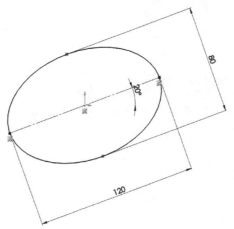

Fig 2-29 Ellipse

2. Create a centerpoint arc slot on the front plane as shown in Fig 2-30. The point A is on the Top plane.

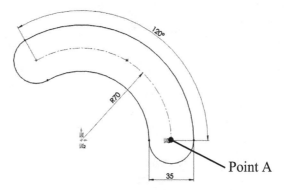

Point A

Fig 2-30 Centerpoint Arc Slot

> ### Applying Angular Dimension by using Three Points
>
> You can apply an angular dimension by selecting three points. Press the Smart Dimension icon, select a corner point and two other points.

3. Create a hexagon on the front plane. The diameter of the outer circle is 100 mm, and the baseline is horizontal. The center of the hexagon is at the origin.

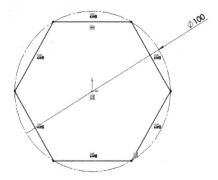

Fig 2-31 Equilateral Hexagon

2.11 Editing Sketch Curves

2.11.1 Trim Entities

By using the Power Trim option of the Trim Entities command, you can trim the sketch

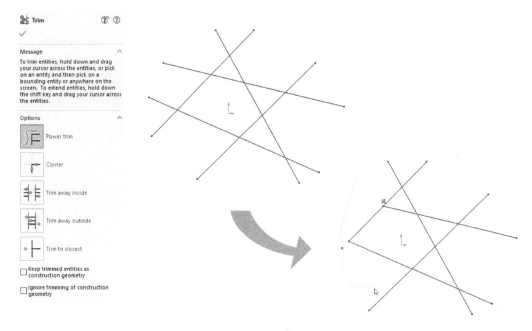

Fig 2-32 Trimming Sketch Entities

curves by left-clicking and dragging the mouse cursor above the curves. If you choose the Trim to closest option, you can select a portion of the curve to trim.

2.11.2 Extend Entities

You can extend a sketch curve up to the next entity.

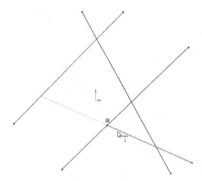

Fig 2-33 Extending Sketch Entity

2.11.3 Offset Entities

You can offset sketch curves. You can use the Cap Ends option as shown in Fig 2-34.

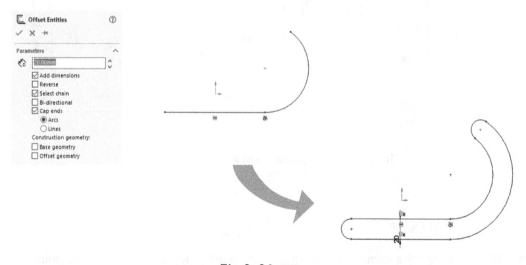

Fig 2-34 Offset

2.11.4 Sketch Fillet

Two curves are connected by using an arc. A side of the connected curves is trimmed out. When the corner being filleted is constrained, you can choose the Keep Constrained Corners option. If you choose the option, the constraint is kept as shown in Fig 2-35. If you unselect the option, the constraint is deleted as shown in Fig 2-36.

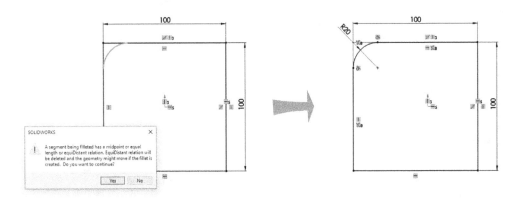

Fig 2-35 With the Keep Constrained Corner Option On

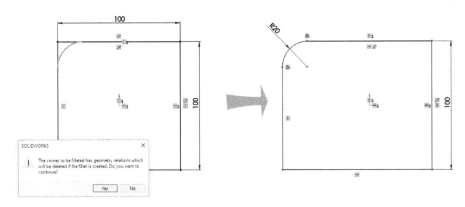

Fig 2-36 With the Keep Constrained Corner Option Off

> **Right-Click**
>
> When you apply a command, the right-click symbol appears at the mouse pointer after selecting the required entities. In this case, you can proceed or finish the command by right-clicking.

2.11.5 Mirror Entities

You can mirror sketch entities according to the following process.

1. Create a centerline.
2. Create sketch entities that are to be mirrored.
3. Click the Mirror Entities icon.
4. Select the sketch entities that are to be mirrored and click the Mirror About selection field.
5. Select the centerline and press OK.

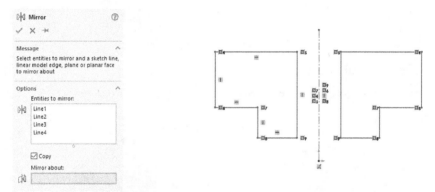

Fig 2-37 Mirroring Sketch Entities

2.11.6 Dynamic Mirror Entities

If you create sketch entities after pressing the Dynamic Mirror Entities icon, the sketch entities are mirrored dynamically. Keep the following process.

1. Press the Dynamic Mirror Entities icon in the Sketch toolbar. You can add the icon by accessing Customize > Commands > Sketch.
2. Select the centerline.
3. Create sketch entities that are to be mirrored.

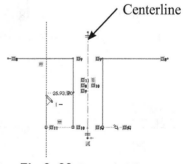

Centerline

If you do not want to mirror sketch entities anymore, you have to turn off the Dynamic Mirror Entities icon.

Fig 2-38 Dynamic Mirror

2.12 Contour

The curves that are selected to extrude or to revolve are called contours. You can select a single closed contour in the intersecting sketch as shown in Fig 2-39.

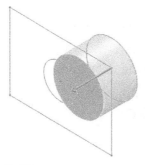

Fig 2-39 Extruding Single Contour

You can select several closed contours by clicking the Selected Contours selection field in the Property Manager. The inner closed contour does not form a geometry as shown in Fig 2-40.

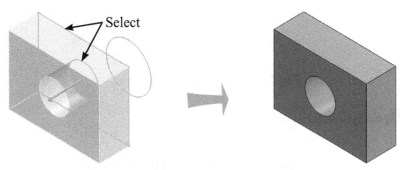

Fig 2-40 Selecting Nested Contour

You can clear the selection of contours or delete a contour by right-clicking in the Selected Contours selection field as shown in Fig 2-41. If you click the selection field, you can add contour either by selecting sketch curves or by selecting the closed area as shown in Fig 2-42.

Fig 2-41 Contours Pop-up Menu

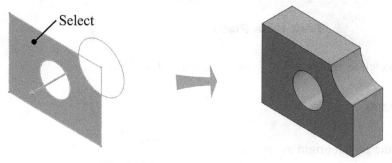

Fig 2-42 Selecting a Closed Contour

Create a link sketch and extrude it by 20 mm as shown in Fig 2-43.

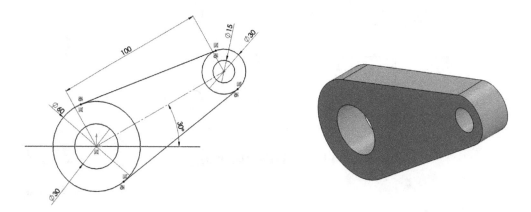

Fig 2-43 Link

END of Exercise

❗ *Do not apply Fix constraint.*

The **Fix** constraint among the geometrical constraints are not used to define the shape of the sketch curves. This constraint is used to fix sketch objects that are imported from another CAD system. Sometimes you may fix some sketch elements temporarily to evaluate the status of constraint of other sketch elements. You have to delete the **Fix** constraint after its temporary use.

Exercise 06 **Four Hole Plate**

Create a sketch as shown in Fig 2-44 and extrude it by 20mm.

Requirements

1. Locate the sketch origin as specified.
2. Apply the Sketch Fillet command.
3. The sketch has to be fully defined.

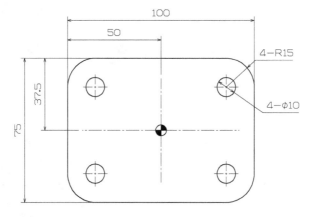

Fig 2-44 Four Hole Plate

END of Exercise

 Symmetric Relation

You can apply the Symmetric relation by creating a centerline and selecting the symmetric curves and the centerline together.

 Display/Delete Relations

You can suppress or delete relations by clicking the Display/Delete Relations icon.

Create a sketch as shown in Fig 2-45 and extrude it by 20mm.

Requirements

1. Locate the sketch origin as specified.
2. The sketch has to be fully defined.

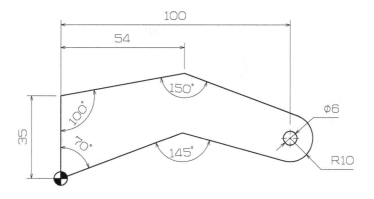

Fig 2-45 Arm

END of Exercise

Applying Constraints in Combination

Two types of constraints are combined to fully define the shape and size of sketch entities. If the geometry changes abruptly by applying a constraint, you will have to undo the constraint and try another constraint. You can drag the sketch curves or points near to the desired location.

Exercise 08 **Sketch with Fillet**

Create a sketch as shown in Fig 2-46 and extrude it by 20mm.

Requirements

1. Locate the sketch origin at the bottom center.
2. The sketch has to be fully defined.

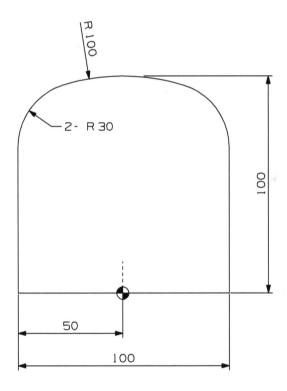

Fig 2-46 A Sketch with Fillet

END of Exercise

Create the sketch shown in Fig 2-47 and extrude it by 20mm.

Requirements

1. Locate the sketch origin as specified.
2. The sketch has to be fully defined.

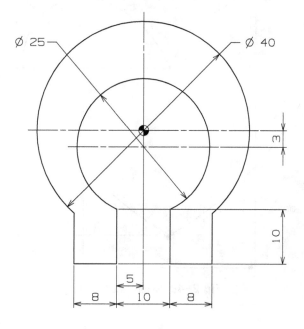

Fig 2-47 Flat Pin

END of Exercise

45

Exercise 10 Creating Symmetric Sketch - 2

Create the sketch shown in Fig 2-48 and extrude it by 20mm.

Requirements

1. Locate the sketch origin as specified.
2. The sketch has to be fully defined.

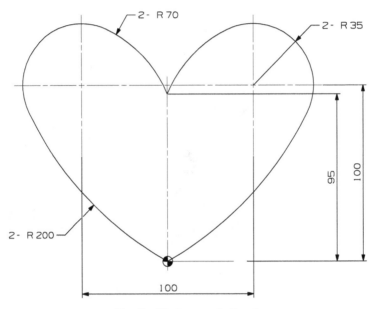

Fig 2-48 Symmetric Sketch

END of Exercise

Create a sketch as shown in Fig 2-49 and extrude it by 20mm.

Requirements

1. Locate the sketch origin as specified.
2. The sketch has to be fully defined.

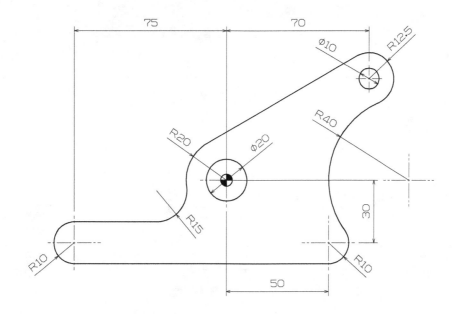

Fig 2-49 Link 1

Flange Cover

Create a sketch as shown in Fig 2-50 and extrude it by 20mm.

Requirements

1. Locate the sketch origin as specified.
2. The sketch has to be fully defined.

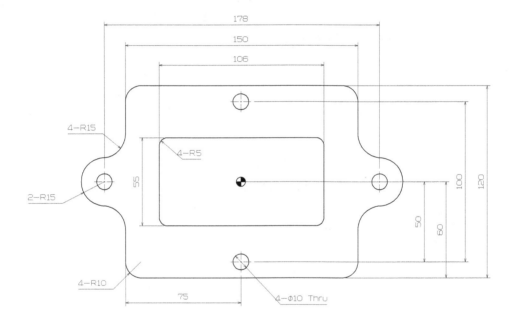

Fig 2-50 Flange Cover

END of Exercise

Create a sketch as shown in Fig 2-51 and extrude it by 20mm.

Requirements

1. Locate the sketch origin as specified.
2. The sketch has to be fully defined.

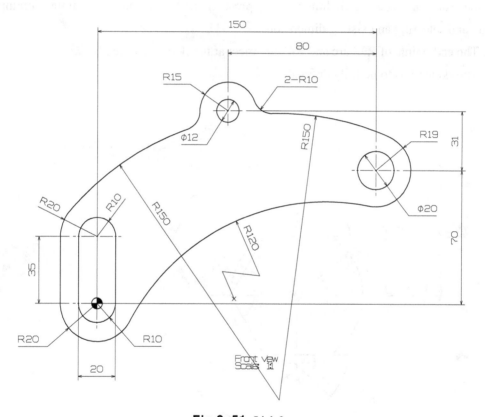

Fig 2-51 Link 2

Spanner Head

Create a sketch as shown in Fig 2-52 and extrude it by 20mm.

Requirements

1. Locate the sketch origin as specified.
2. Link the two dimensions designated by **A** with a formula so that they are always the same. You can link a sketch dimension by pressing the '=' symbol in the dimension input box and selecting an existing dimension.
3. The end points of R28 arc and R45 arc meet at the point specified by **B**.
4. The sketch has to be fully defined.

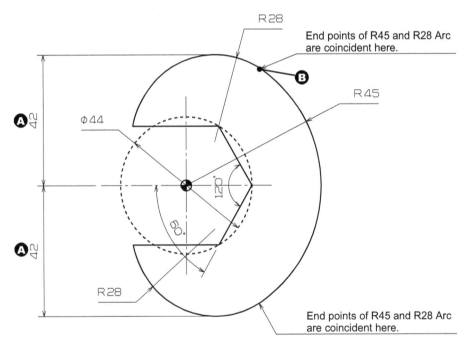

Fig 2-52 Spanner Head

Chapter 3
Extrude, Revolve and Hole Wizard

■ After completing this chapter you will understand

- the characteristics of contours.
- the end conditions.
- how to use the Extrude and Revolve command.
- how to create holes by using the Hole Wizard.

3.1 Extrude

By using the Extruded Boss/Base command, you can create 3D geometry by extruding a closed contour along a direction. The 3D geometry that has a volume is called a solid body. You can merge the extruded geometry to an existing solid body or create it as a new solid body. The Extruded Cut command is activated only when there exists a solid body. The Extruded Cut command removes the existing body by extruding a closed contour.

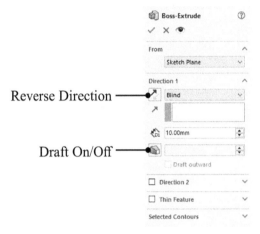

Fig 3-1 Property Manager of Boss-Extrude

3.1.1 From

The From option defines the start location of the extrusion. The start can either be the same as the sketch plane or be a selected plane or vertex.

3.1.2 Direction

You can define Direction 1 and Direction 2 of extrusion. The Direction 2 is opposite to Direction 1. You can reverse Direction 1.

3.1.3 End Condition

The end condition of extrusion can be defined by using a value or by using an existing geometry. This option will be explained in detail in the following section.

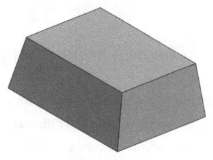

Fig 3-2 Draft

3.1.4 Draft On/Off

You can apply draft to the extrusion as shown in Fig 3-2.

3.1.5 Thin Feature

This option is activated when you are extruding an open contour to create a solid body as shown in Fig 3-3. You can apply the Thin Feature option for a closed contour to create a solid body as shown in Fig 3-4.

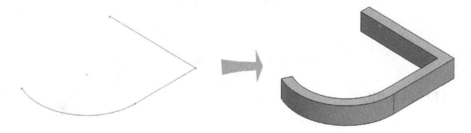

Fig 3-3 A Thin Feature By Using an Open Contour

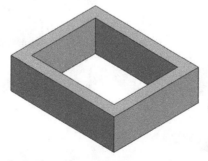

Fig 3-4 A Thin Feature By Using a Closed Contour

3.2 End Condition

There are several types of end conditions for Direction 1 and Direction 2 options.

If you choose Blind, you can enter the depth of extrusion, which is maintained all the time unless you modify the value. Note that you can enter different values for Direction 1 and Direction 2. If you choose Mid Plane, the Direction 2 option is deactivated, and the extrusion is applied for both directions.

If you use a vertex, surface or a body to define the end condition, the depth of the extrusion is updated when the location of the corresponding vertex, surface or body is modified.

Fig 3-5 End Condition

3.2.1 Through All

A contour is extruded through all bodies.

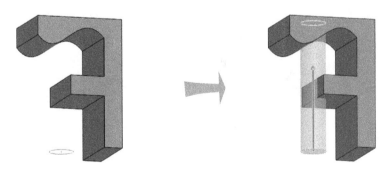

Fig 3-6 End Condition (Through All)

3.2.2 Up To Vertex

A contour is extruded up to a selected vertex. Note that the end of the extrusion is flat.

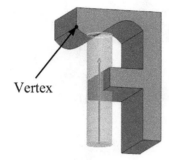

Fig 3-7 End Condition(Up To Vertex)

3.2.3 Up To Surface

A contour is extruded up to a selected surface. Note that the end of the extrusion fits the selected surface.

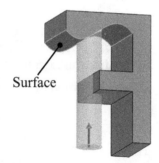

Fig 3-8 End Condition(Up To Surface)

3.2.4 Offset From Surface

A contour is extruded up to the offset of a selected surface. Note that the end of the extrusion is the same as the offset surface.

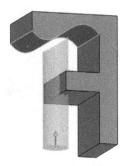

Fig 3-9 End Condition(Offset From Surface)

3.2.5 Up To Body

A Contour is extruded up to a selected solid body.

3.3 Extruded Cut

This command removes an extruded body from an existing solid body. Fig 3-10 shows the result of the extruded cut by using the end condition of Through All.

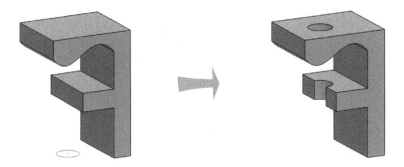

Fig 3-10 Extruded Cut(Through All)

_001.SLDPRT

Creating a 3D Model **Exercise 01**

Create a 3D model as shown in Fig 3-11. The trimetric metric view is shown in View E.

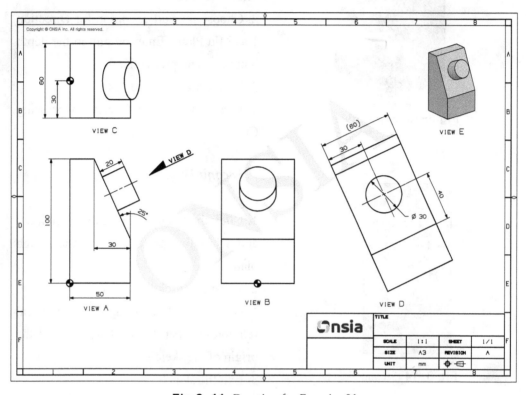

Fig 3-11 Drawing for Exercise 01

Creating a Part and a Sketch

1. Create a part file and create a sketch on the front plane as shown in Fig 3-12.
2. Exit the sketch.
3. Note that the sketch feature is selected. Deselect it by clicking the empty area of the graphics window.

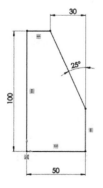

Fig 3-12 Front Sketch

57

Fig 3-13 First Extrusion

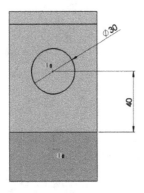

Fig 3-14 Second Sketch

Fig 3-15 Second Extrusion

Extrusion

1. Click the Extruded Boss/Base icon and select the sketch curve.
2. Choose the end condition for Direction 1 as Mid Plane. Enter 60 mm in the depth input box and press OK.
3. Deselect the feature.
4. Display the isometric view by pressing Ctrl + 7.

Second Sketch

1. Click the Sketch icon in the Sketch tab and select the slanted face as the sketch plane.
2. Create a circle as shown in Fig 3-14. Note that you have to apply the Vertical relation between the center point and the origin of the sketch.
3. Exit the sketch.
4. Deselect the sketch feature and display the isometric view.

Second Extrusion

1. Extrude the second sketch and with the Merge Result option.

Save

1. Save the part as the given name.

END of Exercise

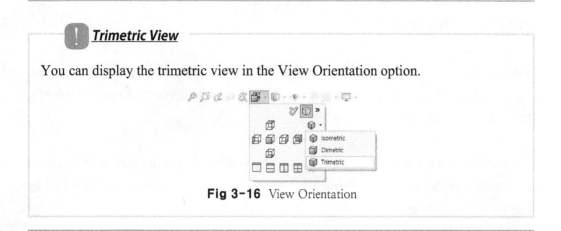

Fig 3-16 View Orientation

---

ch03_002.SLDPRT

Creating a 3D Model | Exercise 02

Condition

1. Feature **Ⓐ** is extruded up to surface **Ⓑ**.

2. Feature **Ⓒ** is cut through all body.

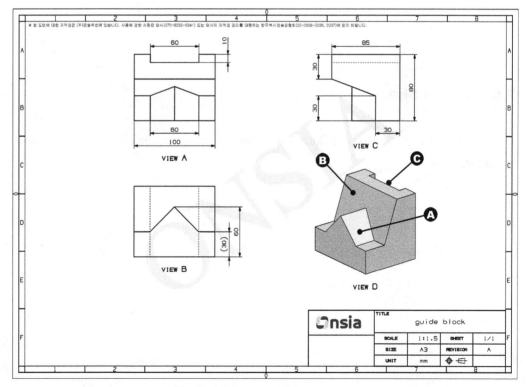

Fig 3-17 Drawing for Exercise 02

3.4 Selecting Contour

You can click the Extruded Boss/Base icon while a sketch feature is selected. If you select a closed sketch, the extruded feature is previewed. Note that if you select an open sketch, a thin feature is created automatically.

The preview is not available when you select a mixed or intersecting sketch. In this case, the contour symbol appears on the mouse pointer. ( ) You can define a closed contour by moving the mouse pointer on a region of the sketch.

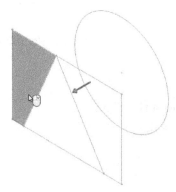

Fig 3-18 Selecting Contour

3.5 Shaded Sketch Contours

If you turn on the Shaded Sketch Contours option in the sketch, the closed sketch contour is shaded.

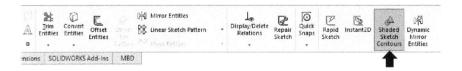

Fig 3-19 Closed Sketch Contours Icon

3.6 Revolve

You can create a revolved feature by revolving a contour about an axis.

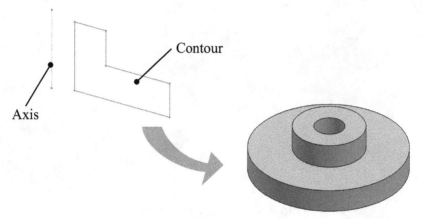

Fig 3-20 Revolved Boss/Base

When you define the contour and axis for a Revolved feature, you have to bear in mind the following characteristics.

① General Rule for Contour and Angle

You can create a solid body by revolving a closed contour. You can select as many contours as you want unless they are intersecting, provided that they are all closed. Total angle of revolution should not exceed 360°.

② Type of Axis of Revolution

You can use the Centerline, standard line or linear edge as the axis of revolution. When you have created an appropriate Centerline, it is selected as the axis automatically. When you are using the standard line as the axis, you have to select the axis in the Axis of Revolution selection field. Fig 3-21 shows creating a revolve feature using the standard line as an axis. Note that you have to select only the rectangle as the profile.

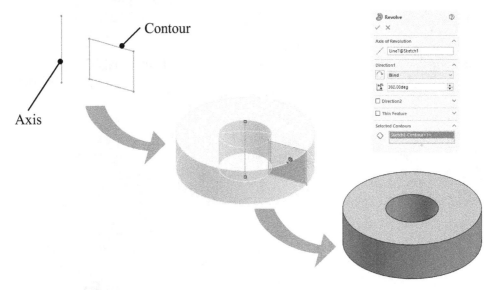

Fig 3-21 Using a Line as an Axis

③ Conditions of Contour and Axis

When you are using an open sketch as a contour of the first revolved feature, you can either close the contour automatically or use the Thin Feature option to create a solid body. If you define an axis of revolution as shown in Fig 3-22, a rebuild error is invoked. Note that the axis of revolution should not be perpendicular to the contour.

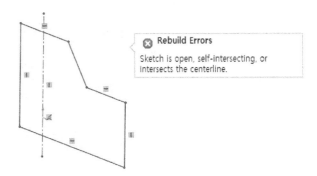

Fig 3-22 Intersecting Axis

3.7 Editing Geometry

You can edit 3D geometry by selecting a feature in the design tree or by selecting an edge or face in the 3D model.

3.7.1 Selecting an Edge in the Model

If you select an edge while the Instant 3D button is ON, a drag handle is available as shown in Fig 3-23, and you can modify the size of the model. Note that you cannot drag it if the selected edge is restrained by other geometry.

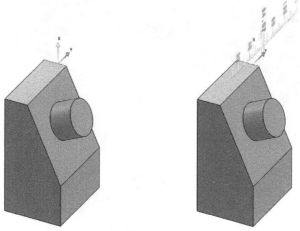

Fig 3-23 Dragging an Edge

3.7.2 Selecting a Face in the Model

If you select a face while the Instant 3D button is ON, a drag handle(Ⓐ in Fig 3-24) and the dimensions to define the selected face appear in the model. You can edit the geometry by dragging the handle. If the face is restrained by other geometry, you cannot drag the face.

You can modify the dimension values by clicking the text and pressing Enter. You can also drag the ball in the dimension line.

If you select the dimension line, the Dimension property manager is invoked as shown in Fig 3-25. You can modify the dimension value or options for dimension line. Note that you have to press the Rebuild button(Fig 3-26) to update the geometry.

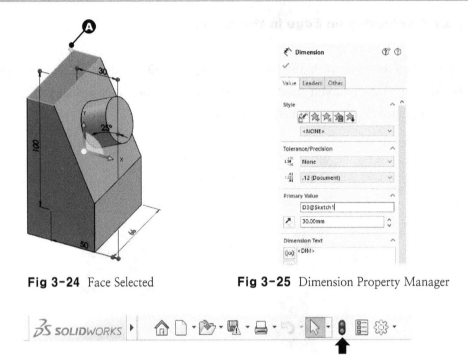

Fig 3-24 Face Selected   **Fig 3-25** Dimension Property Manager

Fig 3-26 Rebuild Icon

3.7.3 Selecting Feature

If you select a feature in the design tree, the dimensions are displayed, and you can modify the dimension value by selecting the dimension text or the dimension line. You can also drag the ball of dimension line to modify the dimension.

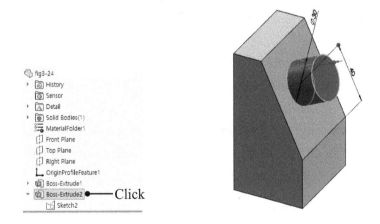

Fig 3-27 Clicking a Feature

Creating the Revolved Boss/Base Feature - 1   Exercise 03

Create a 3D model as shown in Fig 3-28.

1. The sketch has to be fully defined.
2. The fix relation.
3. Use the Revolved Boss/Base command once.

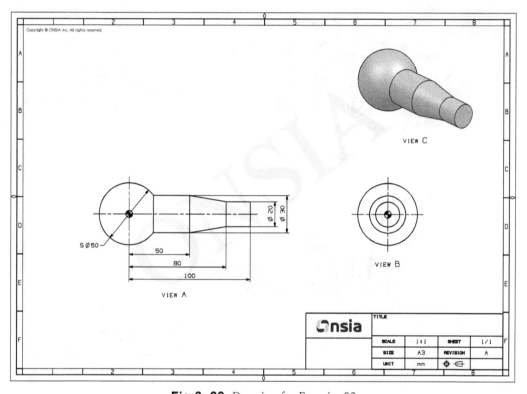

Fig 3-28 Drawing for Exercise 03

END of Exercise

| Exercise 04 | Creating the Revolved Boss/Base Feature - 2 | *ch03_004.SLDPRT* |

Create a 3D model as shown in Fig 3-29.

1. The sketch has to be fully defined.
2. The fix relation.
3. Use the Revolved Boss/Base command once.

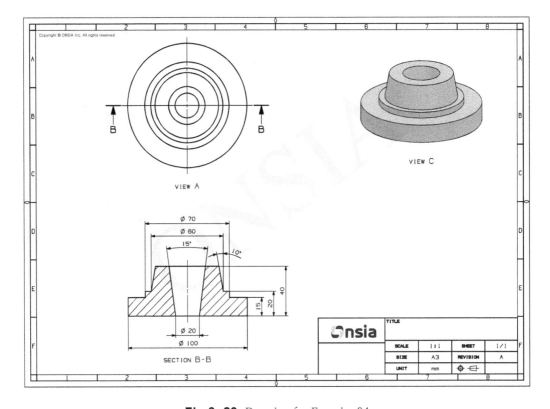

Fig 3-29 Drawing for Exercise 04

END of Exercise

66

3.8 Hole Wizard

You can create standard holes conveniently by using the hole wizard. Keep the following process.

① Click the Hole Wizard icon.
② Select the type of holes in the Type tab and choose other options such as hole type, standard, type, hole specifications, etc.
③ Define the location of the holes in the Positions tab. Select the plane and the base point of the holes.
④ Click OK.

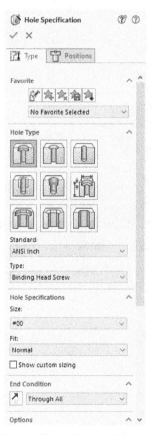

Fig 3-30 Hole Specification
Feature Manager

Note that two sketches are created after creating holes. One is for the section of the holes and the other is for the location of the holes. You can modify each sketch by selecting it in the design tree.

To define the location of the holes, you can either create a sketch or select vertices, the center of a circular edge, or select a point on the hole plane or an edge.

Open the given file and create the counterbored holes by using the Hole Wizard.

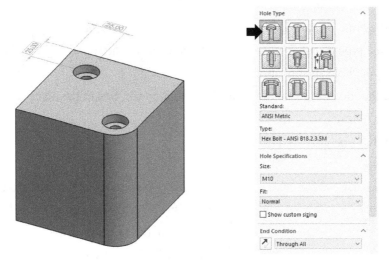

Fig 3-31 Counterborde Hole

END of Exercise

3.9 Boolean Operation between Bodies

If you do not use the Merge Result option when you are creating the second and later extruded or revolved features, the bodies are created as separate ones. Then you can add, subtract or create a common body by using the Combine command in the Solidworks menu > Insert > Features.

Body A in Fig 3-32 is an extruded body by using a rectangle. Body B was created by applying the Shell command after extruding a circle. The Shell command will be explained in the later chapter.

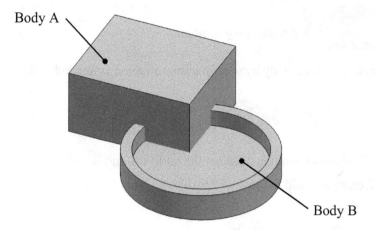

Body A

Body B

Fig 3-32 Two Bodies

3.9.1 Combine - Add

You can add two or more bodies as a single solid
body. If you add Body B to Body A, you can obtain a single solid body as shown in Fig 3-33. You
can distinguish whether the bodies are added or not
by applying the body filter which is explained in the
next page.

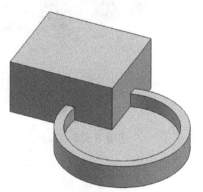

Fig 3-33 Add

3.9.2 Combine - Subtract

You can subtract Body B from Body A as shown in Fig
3-34.

3.9.3 Combine - Common

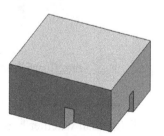

Fig 3-34 Subtract

You can create a common body between Body A and Body
B as shown in Fig 3-35

Fig 3-35 Common

Exercise 06 **Combining Bodies** *ch03_006.SLDPRT*

Let's complete a single body by applying the Combine command to the given part.

Process

1. Apply Combine - Common between the bodies A and B.
2. Apply Combine - Add to the above result and body C.

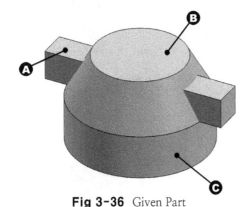

Fig 3-36 Given Part   **Fig 3-37** Completed Model

END of Exercise

 Selection Filter

If you press the F5 key, the selection filter is invoked as shown in Fig 3-38. You can distinguish whether bodies are added or not by pressing the Filter Solid Bodies button.

Fig 3-38 Selection Filter

Let's create a solid model as shown in the drawing. Sketches should be fully defined, and all holes are to be created by using the Hole Wizard.

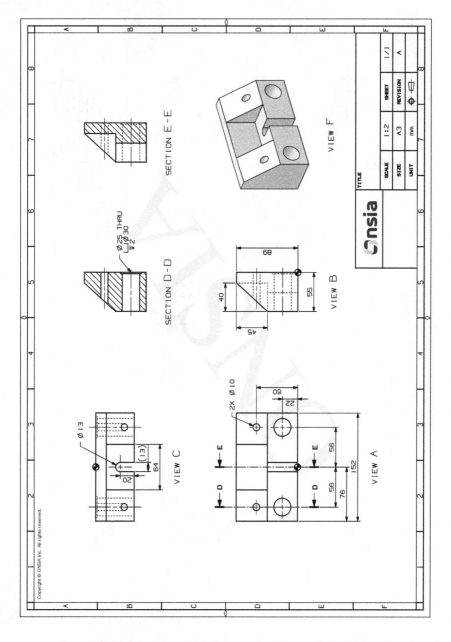

Fig 3-39 Drawing for Exercise 07

Exercise 08   Part Modeling   *ch03_008.SLDPRT*

Let's create a solid model as shown in the drawing. Sketches should be fully defined, and all holes are to be created by using the Hole Wizard.

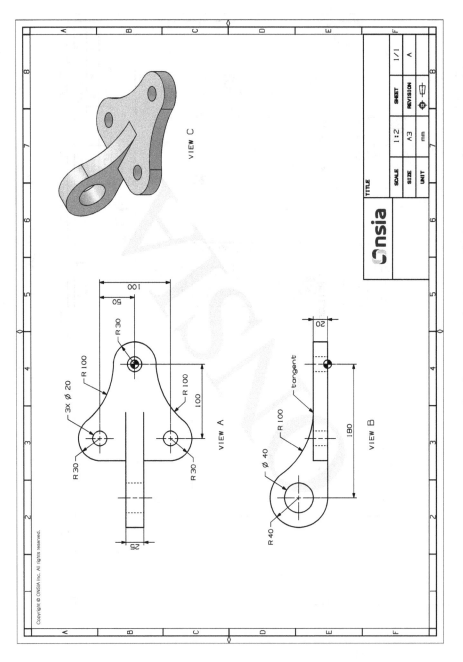

Fig 3-40 Drawing for Exercise 08

Let's create a solid model as shown in the drawing. Sketches should be fully defined, and all holes are to be created by using the Hole Wizard.

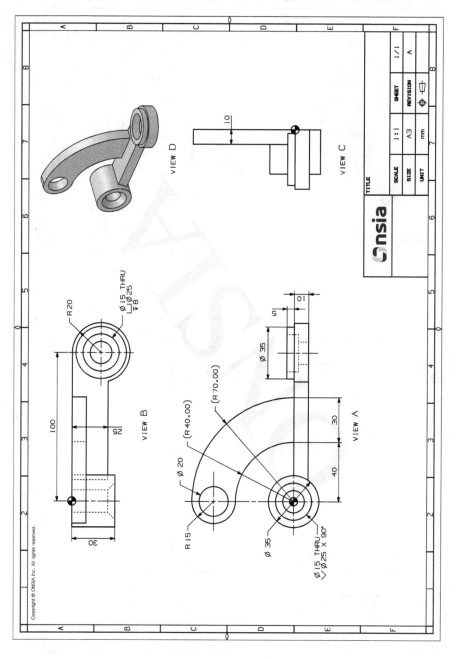

Fig 3-41 Drawing for Exercise 09

Exercise 10 **Part Modeling**   *ch03_010.SLDPRT*

Let's create a solid model as shown in the drawing. Sketches should be fully defined.

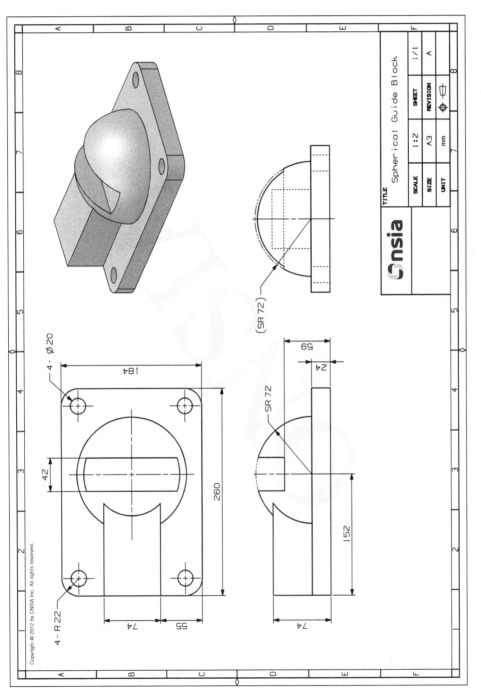

Fig 3-42 Drawing for Exercise 10

Chapter 4
Reference Geometries

■ After completing this chapter you will understand

- the usage of reference geometries.
- how to create reference point, axis, plane and co-ordinate system.
- how to apply reference geometries in creating 3D model.

4.1 Reference Geometries

The 3D model is a volume that consists of vertices, edges and faces. Reference geometries do not constitute a 3D model but are used to define 3D features.

Points, axes and planes are typical types of reference geometry. If there is no plane for a sketch, you will create a reference plane and define a sketch on it. If there are no points or axes to use, you will create reference points or axes, respectively.

The reference geometry is not the purpose of modeling in itself, but an intermediate geometry to define other features. Therefore, after creating reference geometry, you will use it for defining downstream features. Deleting an unused reference geometry will have no impact on the 3D model.

Note that a reference geometry is defined by referencing the existing geometries such as vertices, edges, faces or other reference geometries, and they establish relations with them. If you modify the related geometries, the reference geometry will be updated, and so will be the dependent features.

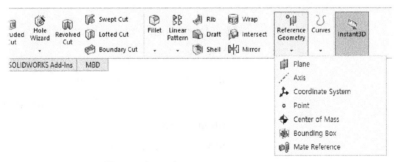

Fig 4-1 Reference Geometries Icon

4.2 Point

The usages of reference points are as follows.

- To set the end condition for extrude or revolve

- To define the location of hole

- To define a reference axis or plane

If you click the Point icon, the Point property manager is invoked as shown in Fig 4-2. You can choose an option for creating a point and select the required geometries.

Fig 4-2 Point Property Manager

- Arc Center: You can define a point at the center of an arc or a circle.

- Center of Face: You can create a point at the center of a face.

- Intersection: You can create a point at the intersection of two curves.

- Projection: You can create a point by projecting an existing point on a face. You have to select a point and a face.

- On Point: You can create a point at the same location as a point a sketch.

- Along curve distance or multiple reference point: You can create a point or multiple points by selecting a curve at the desired location.

Exercise 01   **Creating Reference Points**   *ch04_001.SLDPRT*

1. Create reference points at the center of edges **A** and **B**.
2. Create a point at the center of face **C**.
3. Create five equally spaced points on edge **D**.
4. Create a point at 20 % location on edge **E** as specified by the arrow.

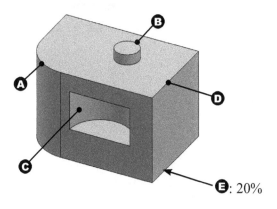

Fig 4-3 Crating Reference Points

END of Exercise

4.3 Axis

The usages of reference axis are as follows.
- To use as a revolution axis of revolve
- To define the direction of move
- To define a reference axis or plane

If you click the Axis icon, the Axis property manager is invoked as shown in Fig 4-4. You can choose an option for creating an axis and select the required geometries.

Fig 4-4 Axis Property Manager

- One Line/Edge/Axis: You can create a new axis by selecting an existing line, edge or axis.
- Two Planes: You can create an intersection axis between two planes.
- Two Points/Vertices: You can create an axis that passes through two points or vertices.
- Cylindrical/Conical Face: You can create an axis at the center axis of a cylindrical or conical face.
- Point and Face/Plane: You can create an axis that passes through a point and normal to a reference plane or a planar face.

Exercise 02   **Creating Reference Axes**   *ch04_002.SLDPRT*

1. Create an axis that passes through vertices **A** and **B**.

2. Create an axis at the center axis of the cylindrical face **C**.

3. Create a point at the center of face **D**, and then create an axis that passes the center point and normal to face **D**.

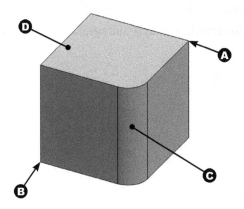

Fig 4-5 Creating Reference Axes

END of Exercise

Let's create a revolved feature with respect to an axis that is an intersection of two planar faces.

Fig 4-6 Model to Create

Creating a Cube and Chamfer

1. Create a 100 mm x 100 mm rectangle on the Top plane and extrude it by 100 mm.

2. Create a 50 mm Distance Distance Symmetric chamfer as shown in Fig 4-7. You can find the Chamfer icon under the Fillet icon. We will learn about the Chamfer command in detail in Chapter 5.

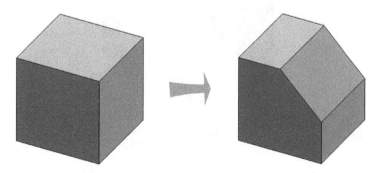

Fig 4-7 Cube with Chamfer

Creating a Circle

Create a 25 mm diameter circle at the center of the planar face as shown in Fig 4-8.

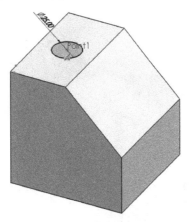

Fig 4-8 Circle

Creating a Reference Axis

Create a reference axis by intersecting face **Ⓐ** and **Ⓑ** as shown in Fig 4-9.

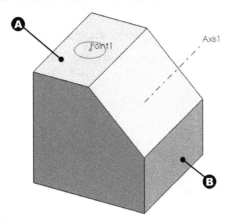

Fig 4-9 Axis

Creating Revolved Boss/Base Feature

1. Click the Revolved Boss/Base icon.
2. Select the circular sketch and the reference axis.
3. Choose Up to Surface as the revolve type and select the face ❸ as shown in Fig 4-10.
4. Select the Merge Result option and press OK.

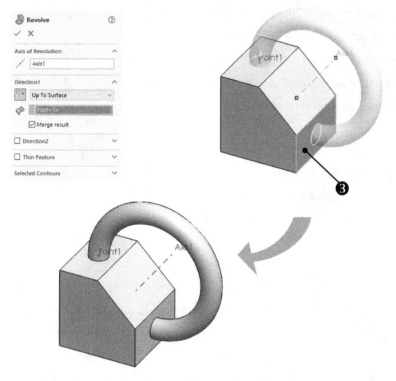

Fig 4-10 Revolved Boss/Base

4.4 Plane

The usages of reference plane are as follows.

- To use as a sketch plane

- To use as a mirror plane

- To define an end condition of the extruded or revolved feature

If you click the Plane icon, the Plane property manager is invoked as shown in Fig 4-11. You can create a reference plane by combining the first, second and third reference objects. You can select a plane, surface, curve, point, axis, plane, etc., as each reference object.

If you select a plane as the first reference, the Plane property manager changes as shown in Fig 4-12. It is fully defined by default because Offset Distance is chosen with a value. No other condition is required to define an offset plane fully.

Fig 4-11 Plane Property Manager

Fig 4-12 Property Manager after Selecting a Plane

There are five constraint options under the first reference: Parallel, Perpendicular, Coincident, Angle, and Offset Distance. If you choose Parallel, Perpendicular or Angle, you have to define the second and/or the third reference to define a plane fully. If you choose Coincident, you can create a plane that is coplanar with the first reference.

Note that you cannot create a plane unless it is not fully defined. An error is encountered if you do not select the second or third reference appropriately.

You can create several planes at the same time when you use the Angle or Offset Distance option. You can create a mid-plane by selecting the first and second references.

Create a 45° slanted plane as shown in Fig 4-13

Fig 4-13 45° Slanted Plane

Process

1. Click the Plane icon.
2. Click the First Reference selection field and select the plane **Ⓐ**, as shown in Fig 4-14.
3. Choose the Angle option and enter 45 deg.
4. Click the Second Reference selection field and select the edge **Ⓑ**, as shown in Fig 4-14.
5. Confirm that the plane is fully defined and click OK.

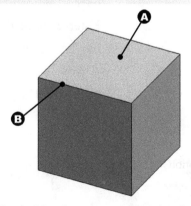

Fig 4-14 The First and Second References

END of Exercise

Exercise 05   **Creating a Tangent Plane**   *ch04_005.SLDPRT*

Let's create a plane that is tangent to a cylindrical surface and passes through a point. The plane is 45° slanted to the Front or Right plane.

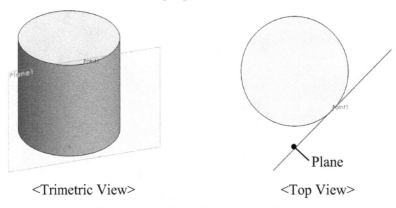

<Trimetric View>   <Top View>

Fig 4-15 A Plane Tangent to Cylinder

Creating a Point

Let's create a point on the circular edge.

1. Open the given part file.
2. Click the Point icon.
3. Choose Along Curve Distance option, enter 0 % and select the upper circular edge. You can identify the 0% location. Enter 25% in the input box and identify the 25% location.
4. Now, enter 12.5% in the input box and click OK. The point is created as shown in Fig 4-17.

Fig 4-16 Point Option

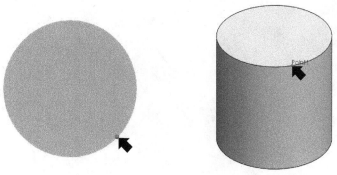

Fig 4-17 Point

Creating Reference Plane

1. Click the Plane icon.
2. Select the cylindrical face as the first reference. Note that Tangent option is available and read the message bar.

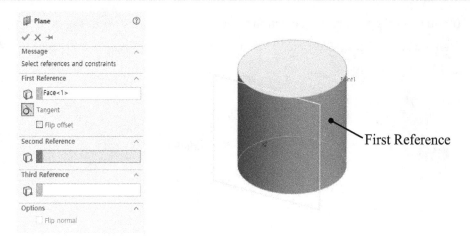

Fig 4-18 First Reference

3. Click the Second Reference selection field and select the point created. Fig 4-19 shows the plane after selecting the point.
4. Confirm that the plane is fully defined and click OK.

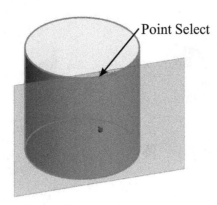

Fig 4-19 Second Reference

END of Exercise

! Selection Filter

If you press the F5 key, the selection filter is invoked as shown in Fig 4-20. You can filter vertices, edges, faces, etc. The shortcuts for vertices, edges and faces are V, E and X, respectively.

Fig 4-20 Selection Filter

4.5 Coordinate System

You can create a new coordinate system in a part and reference it for creating a feature. You can define the origin, X-axis and Y-axis referencing the existing geometries. The coordinate system is updated when the referenced geometries are modified.

ch04_006.SLDPRT   **Coordinate System** **Exercise 06**

Let's create a coordinate system according to the suggested process and verify the parent/child relationships between features.

Creating a Point and an Axis

1. Open the given part.
2. Create a point at the center of the upper face.
3. Create an axis by connecting two vertices as shown in Fig 4-21.

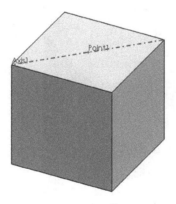

Fig 4-21 Point and Axis

Creating a Coordinate System

1. Click the Coordinate System icon.

2. Select the point as the origin.

3. Select the reference axis as the X-axis.

4. Select the upper face as the Z-axis. The Z-axis is set as the normal to the upper face.

5. Click the Reverse X Axis Direction button if required to create a coordinate system as shown in Fig 4-22.

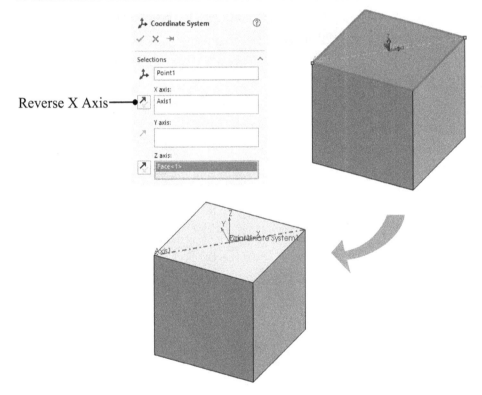

Fig 4-22 Coordinate System

Modifying the Dimension

1. Select the Sketch feature in the design tree. (❶ in Fig 4-23)

2. Select the sketch dimension ❷ as shown in Fig 4-23, modify it into 200 and press Enter.

3. Confirm that the coordinate system is updated.

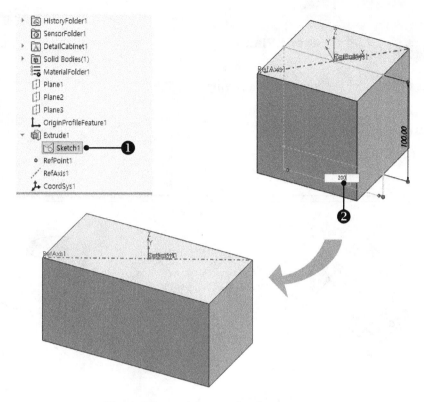

Fig 4-23 Modifying a Sketch Dimension

Verifying the Parent/Child Relationships

Right click on the Coordinate System in the design tree and choose Parent/Child(**Ⓐ** in Fig 4-24) in the pop-up toolbar. You can verify the parent/child relationships as shown in Fig 4-24.

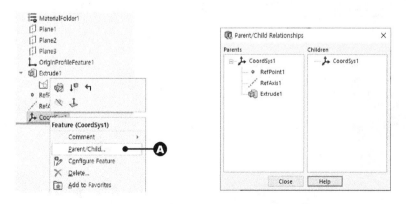

Fig 4-24 Parent/Child Relationships

Exercise 07   **Tangent Plane**   *ch04_007.SLDPRT*

Create a solid model as shown in the drawing.

1. The sketch has to be fully defined.
2. Do not apply any fixed constraint.

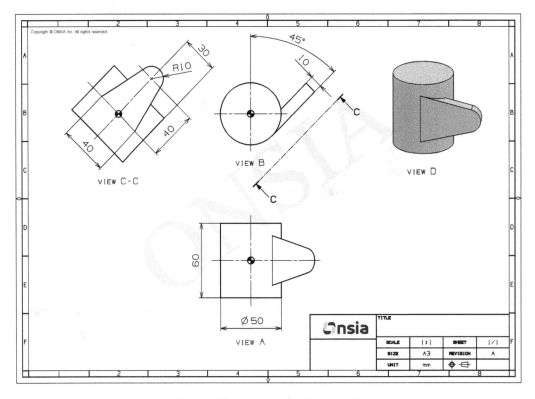

Fig 4-25 Drawing for Exercise 07

Create a solid model as shown in the drawing.

1. The sketch has to be fully defined.
2. Do not apply any fixed constraint.

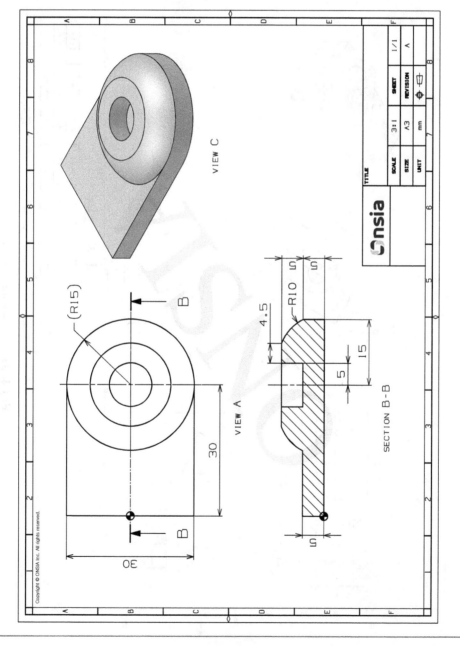

Fig 4-26 Drawing for Exercise 08

93

Slanted Reference Plane   *ch04_009.SLDPRT*

Create a solid model as shown in the drawing.

1. The sketch has to be fully defined without any fixed constraint.
2. Use the Hole Wizard for creating holes.

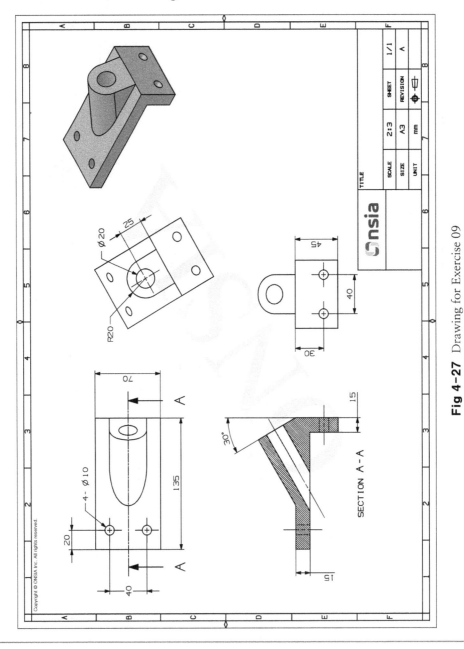

Fig 4-27 Drawing for Exercise 09

Create a solid model as shown in the drawing.

1. The sketch has to be fully defined without any fixed constraint.
2. Use the Hole Wizard for creating holes.

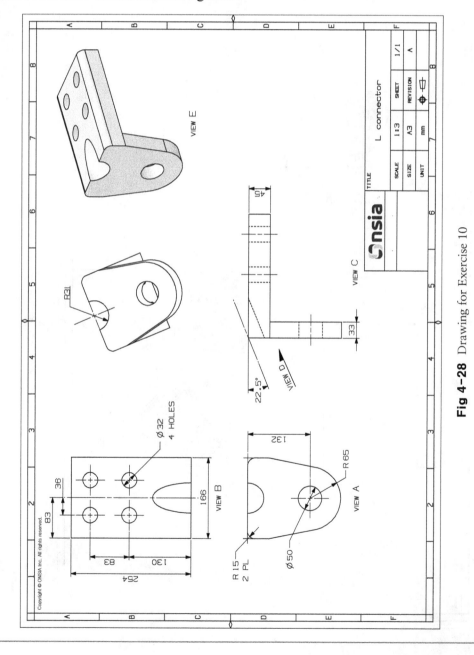

Fig 4-28 Drawing for Exercise 10

Exercise 11 **Slanted Reference Plane** *ch04_011.SLDPRT*

Create a solid model as shown in the drawing.

1. The sketch has to be fully defined without any fixed constraint.
2. Use the Hole Wizard for creating holes.

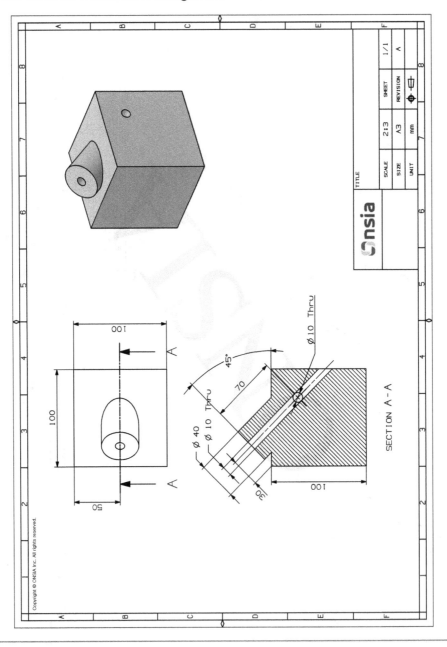

Fig 4-29 Drawing for Exercise 11

Chapter 5
Detailing

■ After completing this chapter you will understand

- the Fillet command.
- the Chamfer command.
- the Draft, Shell, Rib commands.

5.1 Fillet

You can convert sharp edges into smooth edges by using the Fillet command. If you click the Fillet icon, the Fillet property manager is invoked as shown in Fig 5-1.

Four types are available: constant size fillet, variable size fillet, face fillet and full round fillet. If you choose a fillet type, the options are adapted.

5.1.1 Constant Radius Fillet

If you choose the first button, you can apply a constant radius fillet. You can use a symmetric or an asymmetric fillet as shown in Fig 5-2 by selecting an appropriate option in the Fillet Parameters option field.

You can choose Elliptic, Conic Rho or Curvature Continuous in the Profile dropdown.

If you choose the Tangent Propagation option, the tangent connected edges are selected at a click as shown in Fig 5-3.

Fig 5-1 Fillet Property Manager

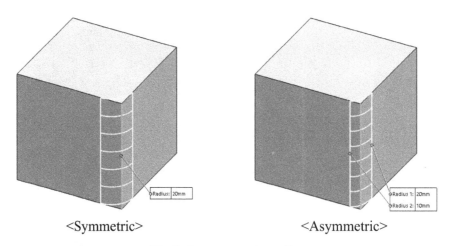

<Symmetric>   <Asymmetric>

Fig 5-2 Constant Size Fillet

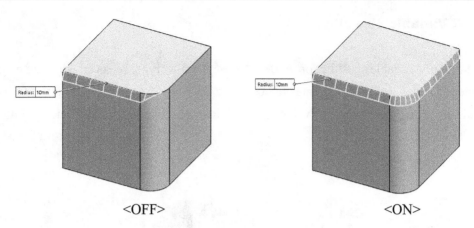

<OFF>   <ON>

Fig 5-3 Tangent Propagation Option

You can apply the setback parameter at the vertices by selecting three and more edged at a time. Click the Setback Vertices selection field (**A** in Fig 5-4) and select the vertices (**B** in Fig 5-4). You can modify the shape of the fillet surface by entering different setback distances and by choosing another profile.

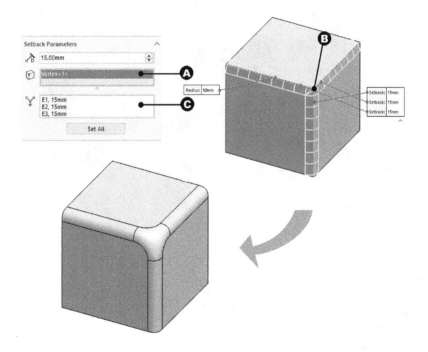

Fig 5-4 Setback Definition

5.1.2 Variable Size Fillet

You can apply variable size fillet on edges. Choose the fillet type, select an edge and enter Number of Instances. You can enter radius value for each vertex by clicking the Unassigned text. You can enter radius values for each instance point by clicking each point.

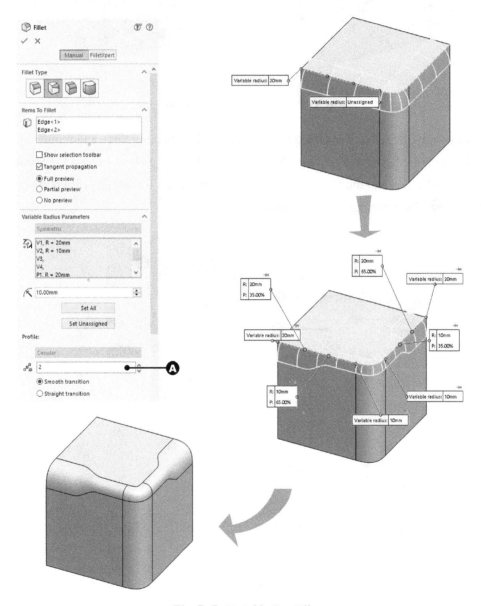

Fig 5-5 Variable Size Fillet

5.1.3 Face Fillet

You can apply fillet between two face sets. This type of fillet is helpful when you cannot apply a fillet on edge or when you apply fillet between two faces that do not meet. Select the face sets, choose fillet profile and parameters, and enter the value. Note that you can select many faces for each face set.

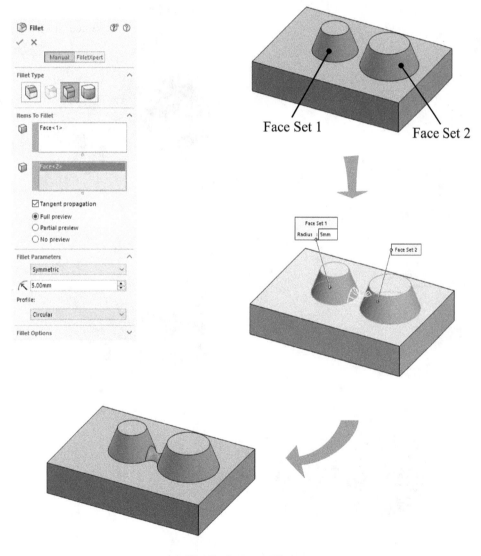

Fig 5-6 Face Fillet

5.1.4 Full Round Fillet

You can apply a fillet that is tangent to three faces. The center face set is removed after applying this type of fillet. Note that you can select many faces for each face set. The only circular profile is available, and you do not need to enter radius because the three tangent conditions define it.

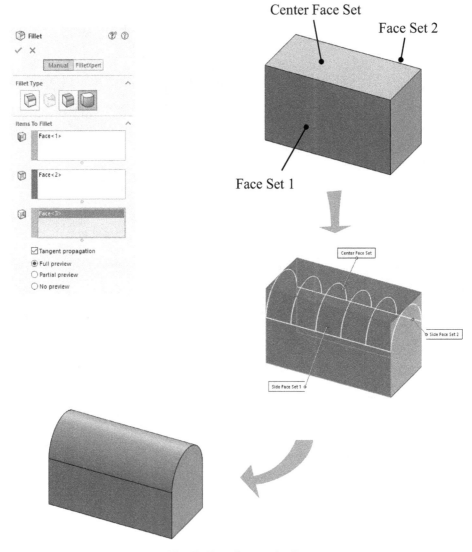

Fig 5-7 Full Round Fillet

Open the given part and create a full round fillet as shown in Fig 5-8.

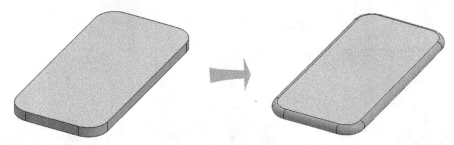

Fig 5-8 Full Round Fillet

> **!** _**Requirement of Full Round Fillet**_
>
> ① Face set 1 and face set 2 have to be separated. If the faces are tangent connected, they have to be considered as being selected at the same time.
> ② The center face set has to connect the faces to fillet.

5.1.5 Guideline for Applying Fillet

Quite often you will not be able to create a satisfactory fillet for complex geometry. The following guidelines outline the steps to create a fillet successfully.

1. Apply the fillet for the larger radius first, and then proceed to the smaller ones.
2. Apply the fillet for the concentrated edges first by selecting the edges at the same time. You can apply setback for this case.
3. Apply fillets one by one, not as a single feature.
4. Apply the fillet for the separate edges first so that the edges to be selected later are tangent connected.

Applying Fillet in Sequence *ch05_002.SLDPRT*

Apply fillet for the given part ch05_002.SLDPRT according to the suggested order.

Case 1: Different radiuses for each edge

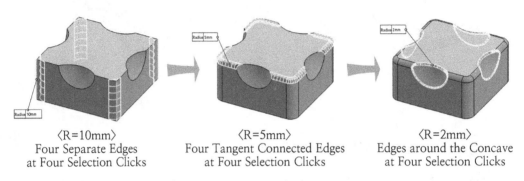

⟨R=10mm⟩
Four Separate Edges
at Four Selection Clicks

⟨R=5mm⟩
Four Tangent Connected Edges
at Four Selection Clicks

⟨R=2mm⟩
Edges around the Concave
at Four Selection Clicks

Fig 5-9 Applying Different Radiuses

Case 2: Same radius for each edge

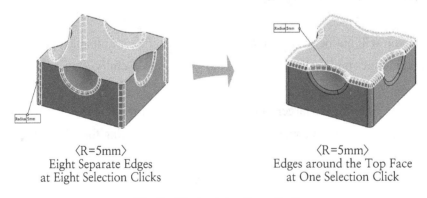

⟨R=5mm⟩
Eight Separate Edges
at Eight Selection Clicks

⟨R=5mm⟩
Edges around the Top Face
at One Selection Click

Fig 5-10 Applying Same Radius

END of Exercise

Applying Fillets in Sequence Exercise 03

Open the file ch05_003.SLDPRT and apply fillets as shown in Fig 5-11. The fillet radius is 3 mm for all edges except the bottom. Apply 10 mm setback distances.

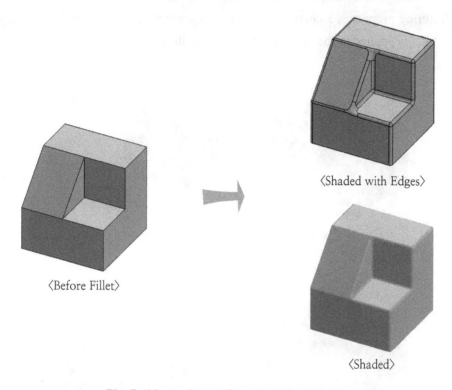

⟨Shaded with Edges⟩

⟨Before Fillet⟩

⟨Shaded⟩

Fig 5-11 Applying Fillet with Setback Option

> ❗ **_Hint!_**
>
> Apply fillet three times as shown in Fig 5-12.
>
>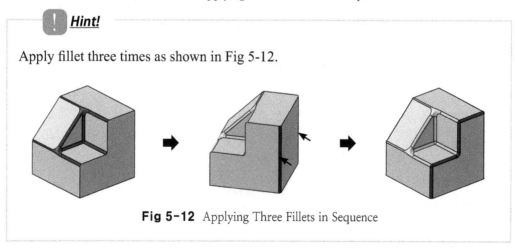
>
> **Fig 5-12** Applying Three Fillets in Sequence

5.2 Chamfer

Sharp edges can be chamfered at a specified angle or by entering a distance from the sharp edge. Material can be removed or added to eliminate the sharp edge of a part. Fig 5-13 shows the case of removing material and Fig 5-14 shows the case of filling material. In manufacturing processes, a chamfer is frequently applied to the part itself. On the other hand, a fillet is applied to the mold and reflected on the part.

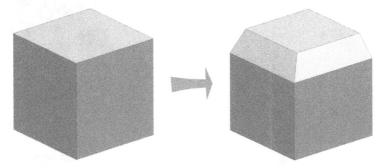

Fig 5-13 Removing Material by Chamfer

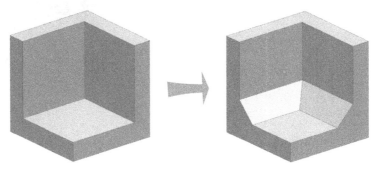

Fig 5-14 Adding Material by Chamfer

Five types of chamfer are available in Solidworks.

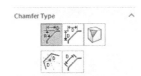

Fig 5-15 Chamfer Type

5.2.1 Angle Distance

You can create a chamfer by entering a distance from an edge along a face and the angle.

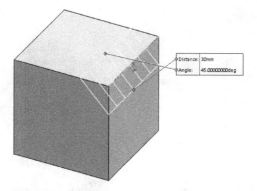

Fig 5-16 Angle Distance Chamfer

5.2.2 Distance Distance

You can enter two distances on the surfaces sharing the edge that is being chamfered. You can enter a symmetric or an asymmetric distance.

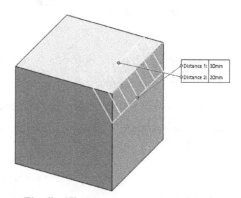

Fig 5-17 Distance Distance Chamfer

5.2.3 Vertex

You can apply a chamfer on a vertex.

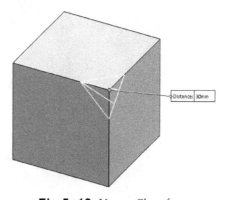

Fig 5-18 Vertex Chamfer

5.2.4 Offset Face

You can apply chamfer by entering offset distances symmetrically or asymmetrically.

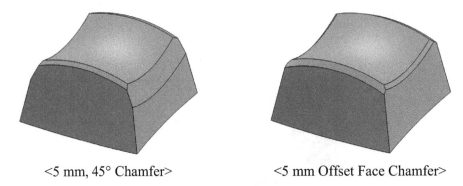

<5 mm, 45° Chamfer>   <5 mm Offset Face Chamfer>

Fig 5-19 Angle Distance vs. Offset Face Chamfer

5.2.5 Face Face

You can apply chamfer between two face sets. This type of chamfer is helpful when you cannot apply a chamfer on edge or when you apply chamfer between two face sets that do not meet. Select the face sets, choose chamfer parameters, and enter the value. Note that you can select many faces for each face set.

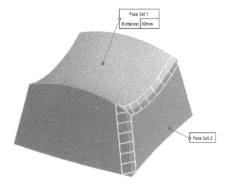

Fig 5-20 Face-Face Chamfer

5.3 Draft

You can apply draft on a face with reference to the pulling direction of the upper mold. If the side face is not guaranteed a proper draft angle, the part cannot be separated from the mold. Fig 5-21 shows the side face before and after draft, where the pulling direction is upward.

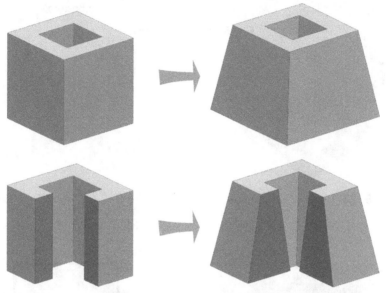

Fig 5-21 Before and After the Draft

Why does the side face of a part have to be slanted? This is a question that arises when you manufacture a part through a mold.

Fig 5-22 shows a part that will be manufactured out of plastic. You will design the upper mold (cavity) and the lower mold (core) as shown in Fig 5-23 and Fig 5-24, respectively.

The two molds are assembled as shown in Fig 5-25 where plastic resin will be injected into the vacant area as designated by ⓐ in Fig 5-25. Temperature is applied to the mold for a while and the resin will become cured as designated by the black area in Fig 5-26. When the part is cured sufficiently, the mold will be opened by pulling the upper mold upward to separate the part from the mold.

However, if the side face of the part or the corresponding face of the mold is parallel to the pulling direction, the side face will be damaged in the area designated by the arrows in Fig 5-27 because of the slip between the faces.

⟨Top⟩   ⟨Bottom⟩

Fig 5-22 Sample Part

Fig 5-23 Upper Mold (Cavity)

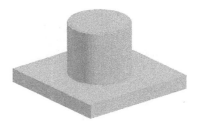

Fig 5-24 Lower Mold (Core)

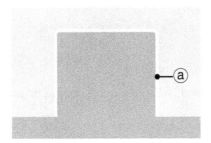

Fig 5-25 Assembled Mold

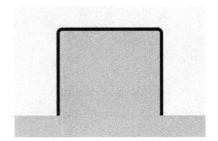

Fig 5-26 Cured Product (Black)

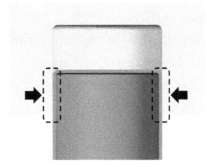

Fig 5-27 Side Face Where Slip Occurs

Damage to the side faces that occurs while the part is separated from the mold can be avoided by applying draft as shown in Fig 5-28. Positive angle draft means that the angle is applied so that the part can be separated easily as shown in Fig 5-29. If you apply a reverse angle draft, you cannot separate the part or the part will be broken.

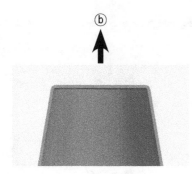

Fig 5-28 Part Applied with Draft Angle   **Fig 5-29** Parting

 ___Direction of Pull (ⓑ in Fig 5-29)___

The direction of movement of the upper mold (cavity) to separate the part from the mold is called a **Pulling Direction**. Sometimes it is called a **Die Direction, Draw Direction** or an **Eject Direction**.

5.3.1 Neutral Plane Draft

The neutral plane does not change after applying a draft. The direction of pull is set normal to the neutral plane.

Exercise 04	Draft - Neutral Plane	ch05_004.SLDPRT

Let's apply draft angle to the faces of given part supposing that the pulling direction and neutral face are as shown in Fig 5-30.

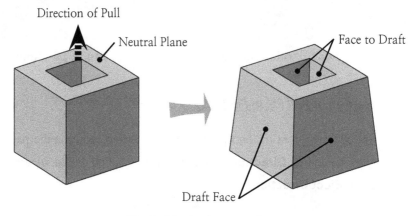

Direction of Pull

Neutral Plane

Face to Draft

Draft Face

Fig 5-30 Applying Draft

Applying Draft

1. Click the Draft icon.

2. Press the Manual button in the Draft property manager.

3. Enter the draft angle.

4. Select the neutral plane. Confirm that the direction of pull is defined as normal to the neutral plane.

5. Select the faces to draft. The total number is 8.

6. Press the OK button.

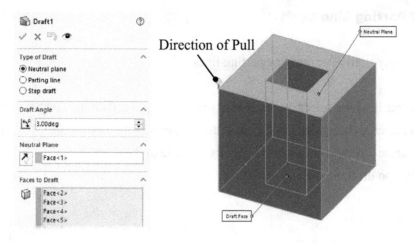

Fig 5-31 Applying Draft

Section View

Click the Section View icon in the quick view toolbar to display the model as shown in Fig 5-32.

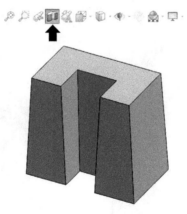

Fig 5-32 Section View

END of Exercise

5.3.2 Parting Line Draft

You can apply draft after creating parting lines.

Click the Parting Line selection field, enter the draft angle and define the direction of pull. You can select a straight edge or a plane to define the direction of pull. If you select a parting line, an arrow is displayed to specify the side of the draft. You can click the Other Face button to draft the other side face.

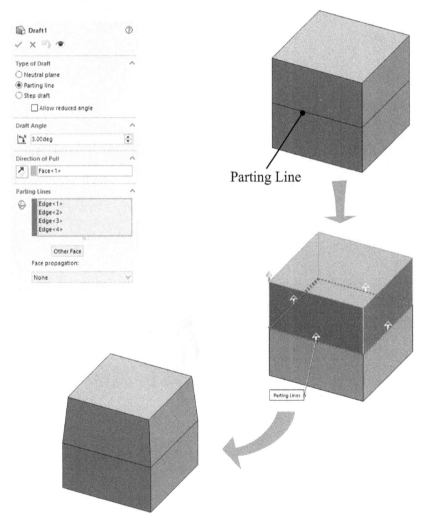

Fig 5-33 Parting Line Draft

5.3.3 Step Draft

A stepped draft is created with the parting lines. Note that you have to select a plane to specify the direction of pull. The plane chosen becomes the neutral plane.

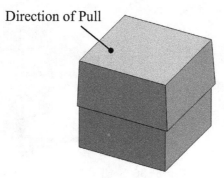

Direction of Pull

Fig 5-34 Step Draft

Fig 5-35 shows the differences between the step draft and parting line draft. The parting line does not change after applying the parting line draft. On the other hand, the parting line can separate in case you have chosen a plane at a distance from the paring line.

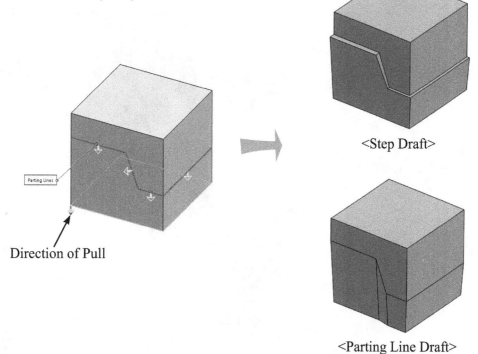

Fig 5-35 Step Draft vs. Parting Line Draft

5.4 Shell

This command hollows out a solid body to create a thin wall. You can either select the faces to remove or not. You can apply either an inward thickness or an outward thickness.

Faces to Remove

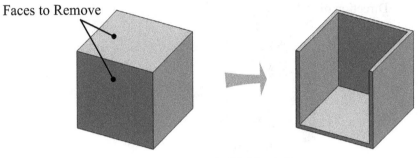

Fig 5-36 Shell

To apply different thicknesses for specific faces, click the Multi-thickness Faces selection field and choose the faces. In Fig 5-37, we removed three faces with 5 mm thickness and applied 52 mm thickness for the bottom face.

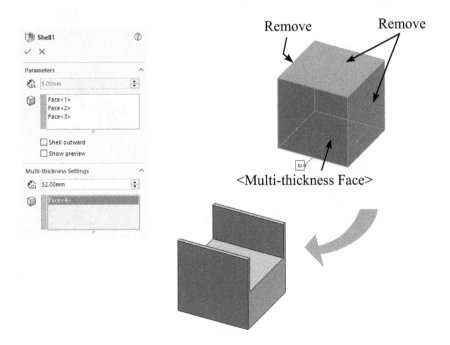

Fig 5-37 Multi-thickness Settings

Note that you can apply the Shell command for the solid body even though it has already been applied. You can create the model shown in Fig 5-38 by applying additional Shell command to the resultant solid body shown in Fig 5-37.

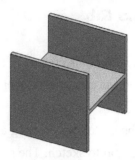

Fig 5-38 Double Shell

If the shell thickness is small enough concerning the existing body, you can apply the Shell command to create the model as shown in Fig 5-39.

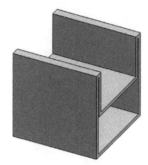

Fig 5-39 Applying Thinner Shell

The left of Fig 5-40 corresponds to the volume of a bottle. If you apply an outward shell, you can create a container with a specific thickness and cavity volume.

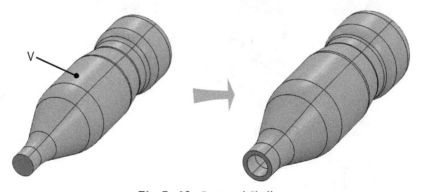

Fig 5-40 Outward Shell

5.5 Rib

A stiffener is created in a weak region of a part to resist against loading. In Solidworks, you can create a stiffener conveniently using the Rib command.

The sketch for creating a rib has to be an open contour. You can create a rib parallel or normal to sketch. The sketch does not need to fit precisely to the existing geometry, but the end of the open contour should be able to be extended to the part geometry.

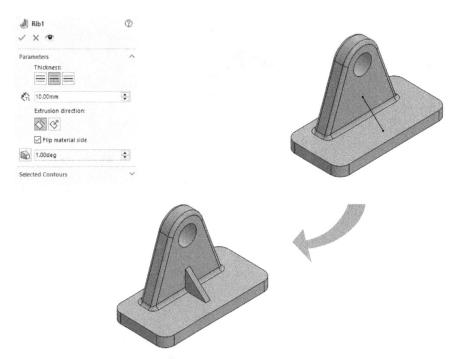

Fig 5-41 A Rib Parallel to Sketch

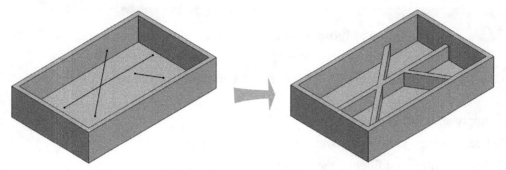

Fig 5-42 A Rib Normal to Sketch

ch05_005.SLDPRT

Open the given file and create a stiffener as shown in Fig 5-43.

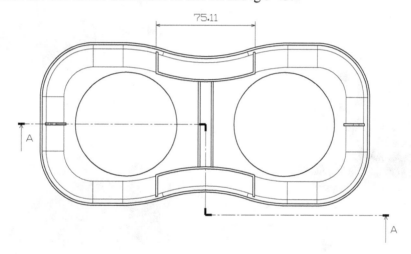

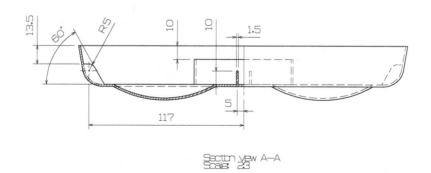

Section view A—A
Scale: 2:3

Fig 5-43 Creating Stiffener

Exercise 06   **Applying Fillet and Shell**   *ch05_006.SLDPRT*

Open the given file and apply fillet and shell according to the following directions.

1. Apply an R5 fillet on the designated edges.
2. Create a 3mm uniform thickness wall removing the bottom face.
3. Apply a full round fillet on the bottom edges.

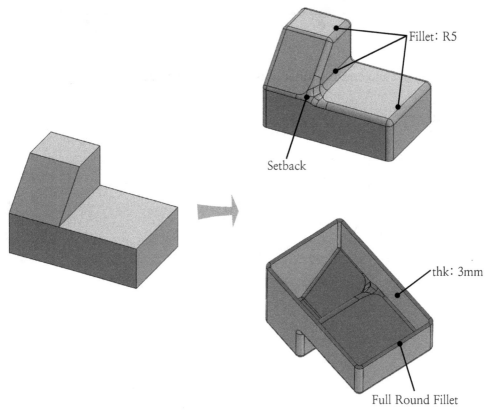

Fig 5-44 Applying Fillet and Shell

END of Exercise

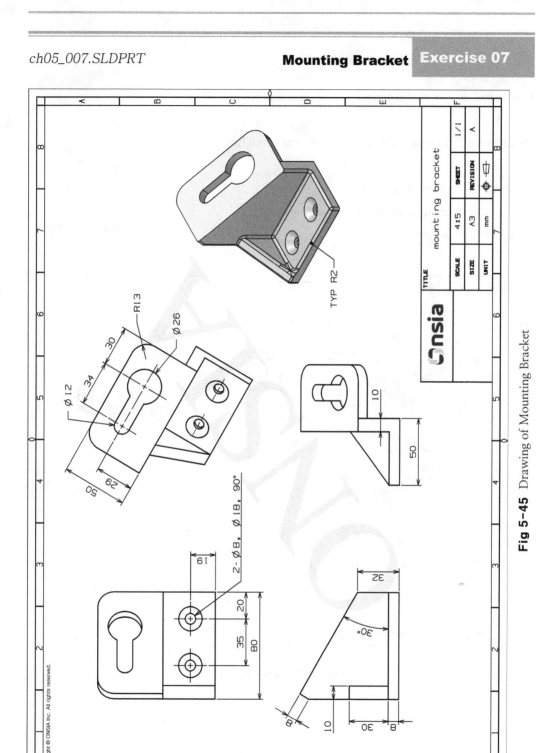

Fig 5-45 Drawing of Mounting Bracket

121

Guide Bracket *ch05_008.SLDPRT*

Create the solid model referring to the drawing in Fig 5-46.

Refer to the following guides for the general modeling procedure.

1. Create all features that add material.

2. Create features that remove material.

3. Apply fillet last.

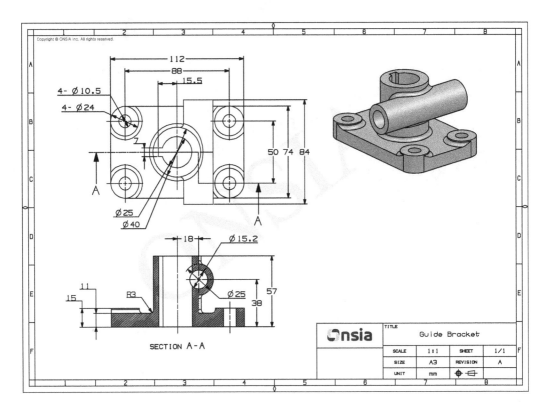

Fig 5-46 Guide Bracket

Chapter 6
Parametric Editing

■ After completing this chapter you will understand

- the parent/child relationships.

- the importance of the feature creation order and how to correct the order.

- how to edit sketch plane.

6.1 Understanding Parametric Editing

We create a 3D model by combining many features. The modeling history is registered in the design tree for each feature. You can edit the features by considering the relations between features.

Fig 6-1 shows a 3D model and its modeling history. We created Sketch 1 and extruded it. Then we defined Sketch 2 on the slanted face and extruded it with the Merge Result option. Hole 1 was created at the center of the circular plane. Note that Sketch 3 and 4 are created automatically by the Hole Wizard. If you edit the angle 45° in Sketch 1 to 60°, the Extrude 2 and Hole 1 are affected by the modification (Fig 6-2). It is called a parent/child relationships. Sketch 2 is a parent feature of Extrude 1, and Extrude 1 is a child feature of Sketch 2.

When you edit features, the parent/child relationships have to be taken into account because the editing can affect children features.

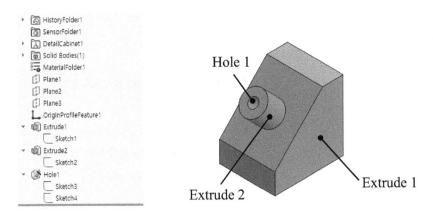

Fig 6-1 3D Model

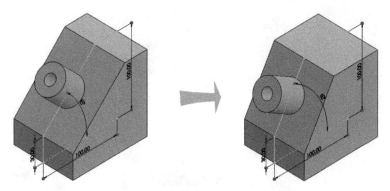

Fig 6-2 Effect of Editing

6.1.1 Parent/Child Relationships

You can examine the parent/child relationships graphically. Right-click on Extrude 2 in the design tree shown in Fig 6-2 and choose Parent/Child. If you double click a feature in the diagram, the parent and children features are refreshed. Note that the top-most feature is the same for each display.

Fig 6-3 Parent/Child Relationships

6.1.2 Deleting a Feature

If you try to delete a feature that has children feature, the Confirm Delete dialog box is invoked as shown in Fig 6-4. You can identify the dependent features in this dialog box. You can either delete the child features or not. If you do not delete the child features, errors take place for the dependent features, and you have to resolve it.

Fig 6-4 Confirm Delete

6.2 Editing a Sketch

You can consider the following three approaches for editing sketch.

① Leave the sketch curves intact and modify the sketch dimensions or constraints. You can delete the constraints and re-define new ones.

② Delete sketch curves or create new curves and fully define the curves.

③ Change the sketch plane.

You will take the first approach in most cases. The second approach may be taken when the first approach is not sufficient to obtain the desired sketch. The third approach is taken when you have to move the sketch plane to another plane.

6.2.1 Editing Sketch Dimensions or Relations

You can edit the dimensions by clicking a sketch feature. Refer to "3.7 Editing Geometry" for detail. If you want to modify relations, right-click on a sketch feature and choose Edit Sketch in the pop-up menu. Press Ctrl + 8 to align the sketch plane. You can delete the relation symbols and define new relations. You can use the Display/Delete Relations icon.

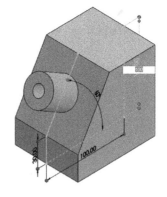

Fig 6-5 Editing Sketch Dimension

6.2.2 Editing Sketch Curves

When you delete or create new sketch curves, you have to bear in mind that the modification can take severe effects on the children features. However, it is recommended to understand the mechanism of editing sketch curves and try it. It would be better for you to resolve the effects of modification rather than deleting all children features.

6.2.3 Editing Sketch Plane

You can edit the sketch plane by clicking or right-clicking on a sketch feature and selecting Edit Sketch Plane in the pop-up menu.

Note that other sketch objects such as dimensions and relations are maintained after changing the sketch plane. Therefore, you would have to correct errors in dimensioning or constraining. You may even have to modify the normal direction of the sketch plane.

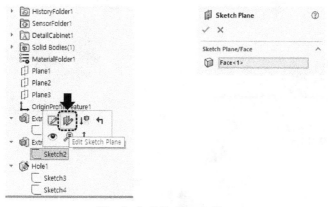

Fig 6-6 Edit Sketch Plane

6.3 Modeling Order

6.3.1 Rollback and Roll Forward

Features are registered in order in the design tree, but you cannot understand the modeling process by examining only the design tree. If you roll back the modeling history to a specific feature step, the effect of the feature becomes clearer and clearer. You can roll forward, roll to previous or roll to end by right-clicking on a feature after rollback.

You can also rollback the modeling history by dragging the rollback bar.

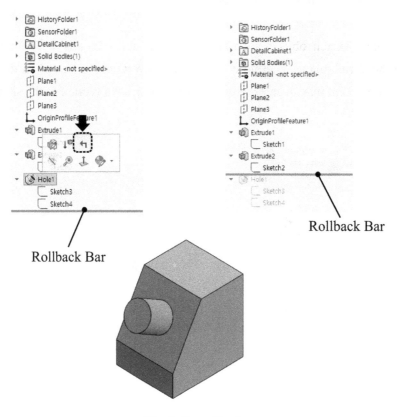

Fig 6-7 Rollback

6.3.2 Reordering

The modeling order plays an essential role in constructing 3D model effectively. A wrong order may cause unnecessary recursive features. In some cases, you may not be able to build the desired shape.

Fig 6-8 requires additional fillets to the internal edges to obtain a uniform thickness. If you drag the Shell feature after the Fillet2 feature, the extra fillets to the inner edges become unnecessary.

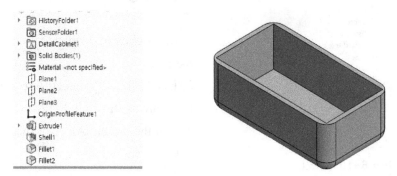

Fig 6-8 Wrong Shell Order

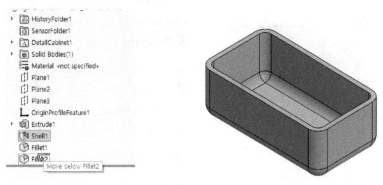

Fig 6-9 Reordering

6.3.3 Inserting Features

Reordering features by drag and drop is available between features that do not have parent/child relationships. When you cannot reorder features through drag and drop, you need to delete the features with wrong orders and build the features after rollback.

Exercise 01   **Editing Sketch Curves**   *ch06_001.SLDPRT*

In this exercise, we will practice the following modeling techniques.

1. Delete a sketch curve and create a new one.
2. Insert a reference plane after the desired feature and before the feature to use it.
3. Change the sketch plane with the inserted reference plane.

Fig 6-10 Sketch to Edit

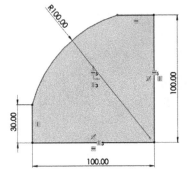

Fig 6-11 Edited Sketch

Deleting Sketch Curve and Adding

1. Right-click on Sketch1 and choose Edit Sketch.
2. Delete the 45° slanted line and add an R100 arc as shown in Fig 6-11.
3. Exit the sketch. An error message is invoked as shown in Fig 6-12.
4. Press Continue. The reasons for errors and suggestions to deal with the errors are displayed as shown in Fig 6-13.
5. Press the Close button.

If you place the mouse pointer on the feature with error, the error message is displayed as shown in Fig 6-14. The sketch plane is missing.

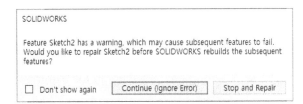

Fig 6-12 Error Message

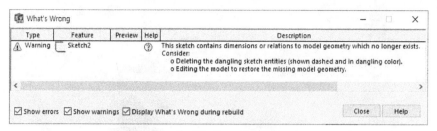

Fig 6-13 Error Message

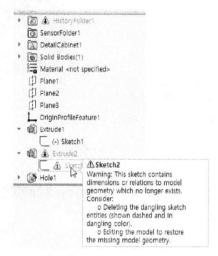

Fig 6-14 Error Message

Fig 6-15 Rollback

Adding a Reference Plane

A slanted reference plane is required on which to place the sketch. We need to roll-back before Sketch2.

1. Drag the rollback bar before Extrude2.
2. Click Reference Geometry > Plane icon and choose the first and second references as shown in Fig 6-16.
3. Choose the Flip Normal option and press OK.
4. Roll to the end of history.

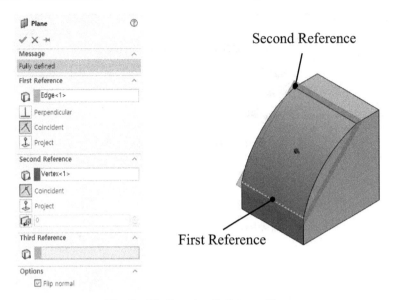

Fig 6-16 Creating Reference Plane

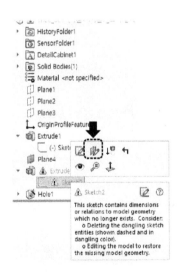

Fig 6-17 Editing Sketch Plane

Editing Sketch Plane

1. Select Sketch2 in the design tree and choose Edit Sketch Plane.

2. Select the reference plane created in Fig 6-16.

3. Press Continue in the error message box shown in Fig 6-18.

4. Press Close in the error message box shown in Fig 6-19.

The error is not resolved because there exists a relation not up to date.

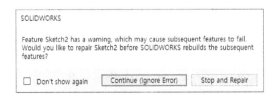

Fig 6-18 Error Message

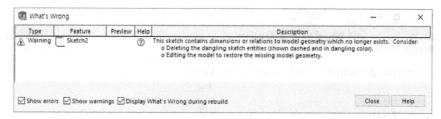

Fig 6-19 Error Message

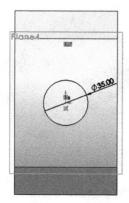

Fig 6-20 Remove Relation

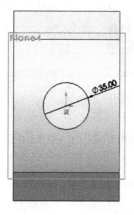

Fig 6-21 Fully Defined

Editing Relations

1. Right-click on Sketch2 and choose Edit Sketch.
2. Press Ctrl + 8 to align sketch.
3. Delete the yellow relation symbols and make sure that the sketch is fully defined.
4. Exit the sketch.

You can see that all errors are resolved in the design tree. Fig 6-22 shows the completed model.

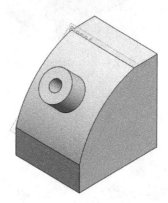

Fig 6-22 Completed Model

END of Exercise

Exercise 02 **Modeling Order** *ch06_002.SLDPRT*

In this exercise, we will edit the model as follows.

1. Reorder a feature.
2. Insert a feature considering the modeling order.

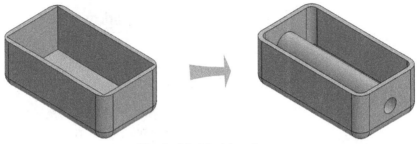

Fig 6-23 Model to Create

Fig 6-24 Reordered Feature

Reordering Feature

1. Open the given part and confirm that the thickness is not uniform.
2. Drag Shell1 after Fillet2.
3. Make sure that the thickness is modified to be uniform.

Rollback and Adding a Hole

We need to add a hole before Shell1 to create a model shown in Fig 6-23.

1. Drag the rollback bar before Fillet1.
2. Create a sketch point as shown in Fig 6-25, and define it fully. You can create a reference point.
3. Create an M12 screw clearance hole as shown in Fig 6-26.

Fig 6-25 Point

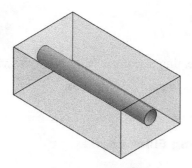

Fig 6-26 Hole

Fig 6-27 Update

Update

1. Move the rollback bar up to the end of history.

Fig 6-28 shows the completed model.

Fig 6-28 Completed Model

6.4 Editing Feature

You can edit options for creating a feature. Modifying the numerical values is relatively simple than reselecting items to apply commands.

Editing Fillet Edges *ch06_003.SLDPRT*

Let's modify the edges of fillets and resolve the errors encountered by deselecting and/or selecting new edges. We will not delete the fillet feature, but modify the existing one.

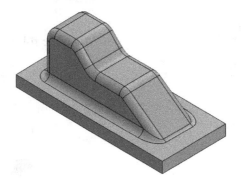

Fig 6-29 Part for Exercise

Reviewing Modeling History

1. Open the given part.
2. Review the modeling history by moving the rollback bar back and forth.
3. Move the rollback bar to the end.

Editing Sketch

1. Click Sketch2 in the design tree and choose Edit Sketch in the pop-up menu.
2. Press Ctrl + 8 and delete the curve **Ⓐ** shown in Fig 6-30.
3. Press Yes in the information box shown in Fig 6-31.
4. Add the sketch curve as shown in Fig 6-32. We skip defining the sketch fully.
5. Exit the sketch.

The part is updated as shown in Fig 6-33. Note that error takes place in Fillet1.

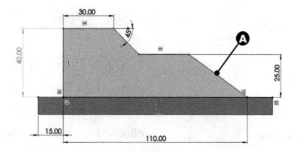

Fig 6-30 Sketch before Edit

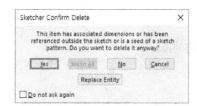

Fig 6-31 Information

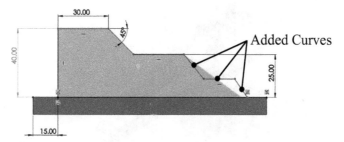

Fig 6-32 Sketch after Edit

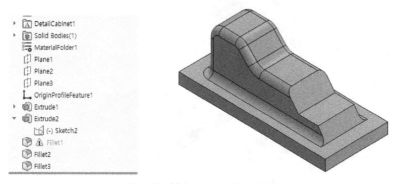

Fig 6-33 Updated Model

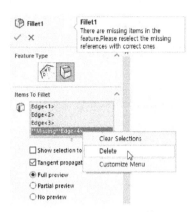

Fig 6-34 Delete Option

Editing Fillet

1. Click Fillet1 in the design tree and choose Edit Feature.

2. Right-click on the missing item and choose Delete as shown in Fig 6-34.

3. Select the additional edges as shown in Fig 6-35.

4. Press OK in the Fillet property manager.

Fig 6-36 shows the completed model.

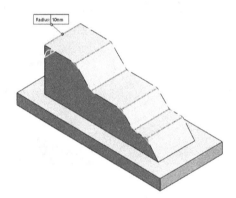

Fig 6-35 Selecting Edges

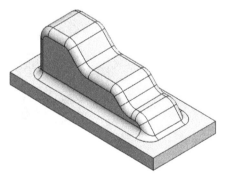

Fig 6-36 Completed Model

Let's modify contours of the extruded features considering the modeling order and add features to correct errors in shape. Refer to the drawing on Page 122.

Consideration

The drilling process suggests that we have to create holes after merging extruded features without holes.

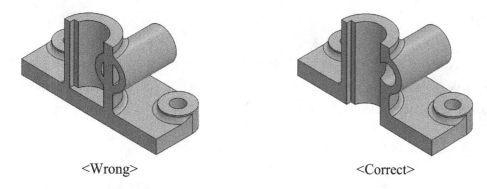

<Wrong>   <Correct>

Fig 6-37 Section Cut

Step 1

Referring to Fig 6-38 and Fig 6-39, edit the contour for Extrude2 such that the inner curves are not included.

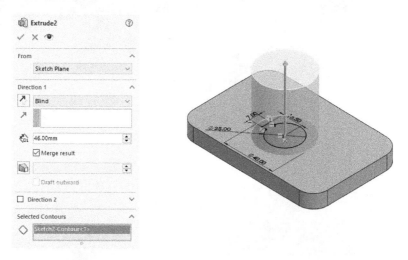

Fig 6-38 Editing Profile for Extrude2

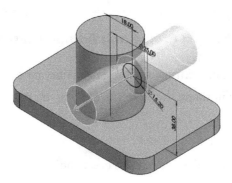

Fig 6-39 Editing Profile for Extrude3

Step 2

Rollback after Extrude3 and add the Extruded Cut feature as shown in Fig 6-40. Note that you have to show the corresponding sketches. Rollback is not required, but it is recommended to collect related features.

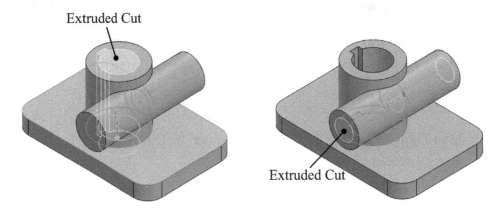

Extruded Cut

Extruded Cut

Fig 6-40 Extruded Cut

END of Exercise

Inserting Features and Resolving Error | Exercise 05

Open the given part and insert the extruded cut feature considering the modeling order and resolve the encountered errors.

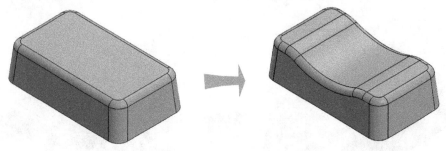

Fig 6-41 Before and After Editing

Step 1

Rollback after Boss-Extrude1, create a sketch on the Top plane and cut as shown in Fig 6-42.

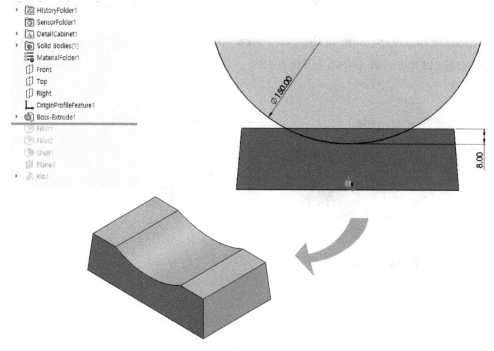

Fig 6-42 Extruded Cut

Step 2

1. Update to the end of history and review the result.
2. Rollback to Fillet1 and add another R30 fillet as shown in Fig 6-43.
3. Update to the end of history and review the result.

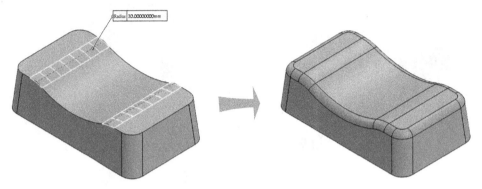

Fig 6-43 Adding Fillet

Right-click on the part name and choose Top Level Transparency in the pop-up menu to display the model as shown in Fig 6-44.

Click the Section View icon in the quick view toolbar. You can set two cut sections to display the cut model as shown in Fig 6-45.

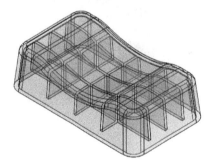

Fig 6-44 Transparency

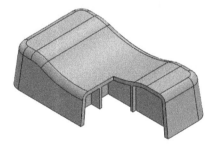

Fig 6-45 Two Cut Sections

END of Exercise

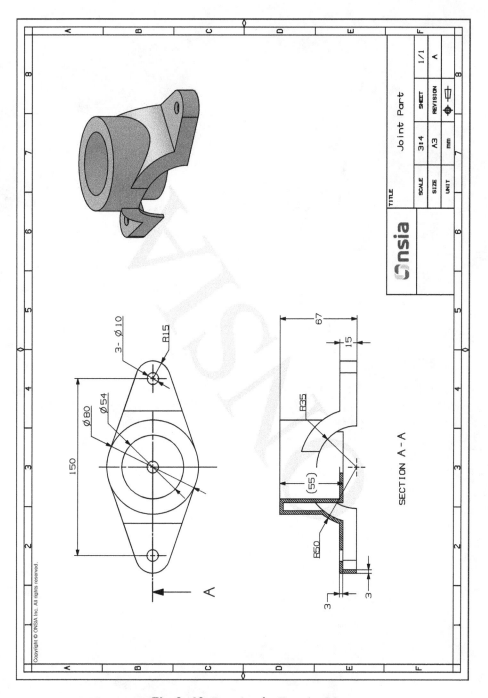

Fig 6-46 Drawing for Exercise 06

143

This page left blank intentionally.

Chapter 7

Copy of Objects and Features

■ After completing this chapter you will understand

- the advantages of copying features and objects.
- how to create linear pattern, circular pattern, mirror and sketch driven pattern.

7.1 Introduction

Repeating the same modeling process several times is time consuming and tedious. Once a feature or object is created, you can escape from tiresome modeling repetition by applying commands that copy features or objects. Moreover, you can modify the result of the copy by changing the copy options. Fig 7-1 shows copying a hole to create four holes. The number of instances can be changed to eight as shown in Fig 7-2 by modifying the corresponding copy option. If the size of the instanced hole is changed, the sizes of all instances are updated.

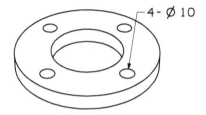

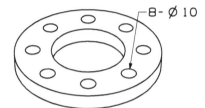

Fig 7-1 Four Holes   **Fig 7-2** Eight Holes

7.2 Classifying Copy Commands

You can choose the required command correctly by remembering the following two guidelines.

① Types of copy source: Which to copy?
② Method of copy: How to copy?

7.2.1 Method to Copy

Fig 7-3 shows the copy commands in Solidworks. In this textbook, we will learn how to use the Linear Pattern, Circular Pattern, Mirror and Sketch Driven Pattern commands.

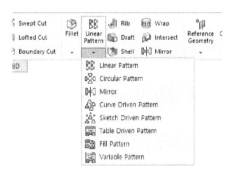

Fig 7-3 Copy Commands

7.2.2 Source of Copy

You can select features, faces and bodies as the source of copy. Fig 7-4 shows the options that allow you to select the source separately. You can select as many features and faces as you want. When you select Bodies option, you are copying bodies, the Features and Faces option is not available.

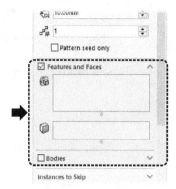

Fig 7-4 Source of Copy

Note that you cannot copy all types of features. You cannot copy the features such as sketch and reference geometry which are not the geometry in itself. You cannot copy the fillet and shell features independently. When you are copying faces, the instance has to be able to build the same filling or removing geometry as the source.

7.3 Linear Pattern

You can copy bodies, features or faces along two directions. You can specify the number of instances for each direction.

Ⓐ: You can select a straight edge or face to specify the direction.
Ⓑ: This option specifies the placement method.
- Spacing and Instances: You can enter spacing between instances and the total number of instances.
- Up to Reference: The instance is placed at the selected reference such as points and planes.
Ⓒ: You can specify the instances to skip.
Ⓓ: You can define irregular spacing between instances.

Fig 7-5 Linear Pattern Property Manager

147

Exercise 01 **Sew Surface**   *ch07_001.SLDPRT*

Let's create a linear pattern along two directions as shown in Fig 7-6.

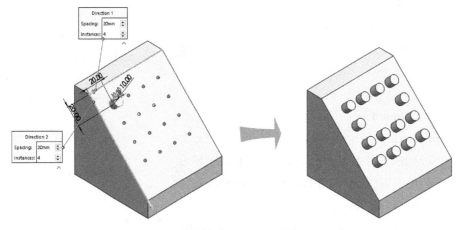

Fig 7-6 Linear Pattern

END of Exercise

7.4 Circular Pattern

You can copy bodies, features or faces by rotating with respect to an axis.

A: Specify the direction of rotation. You can select a straight edge or an axis.

B: This option specifies the placement method.
- Instance Spacing: You can enter angular spacing between instances and the total number of instances.
- Equal Spacing: Specified number of instance is equally spaced in a total specified angle.

Fig 7-7 Circular Pattern Property Manager

Open the given part and create a circular pattern according to the suggested step.

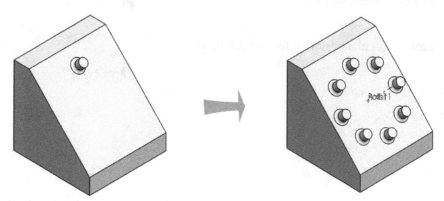

Fig 7-8 Circular Pattern

Step 1

1. Create a point at the center of the slanted face.
2. Create an axis that passes through the point and normal to the slanted face.

Step 2

Pattern the Extrude2 and Fillet1 features as shown in Fig 7-10.

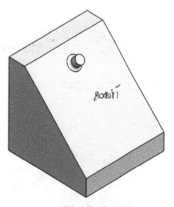

Fig 7-9 Axis

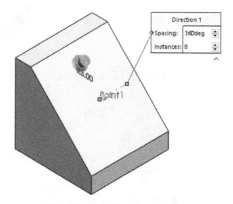

Fig 7-10 Circular Pattern

END of Exercise

7.5 Mirror

You can mirror features, faces or bodies with respect to a planar face or a reference plane.

A: You can select planar mirror face or reference plane.

B: You can select features, faces or bodies as the source of mirrored copy.

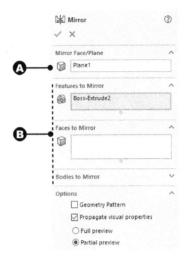

Fig 7-11 Mirror Property Manager

Mirror and Modeling Order   *ch07_003.SLDPRT*

Open the given part and proceed the modeling process according to the suggested process.

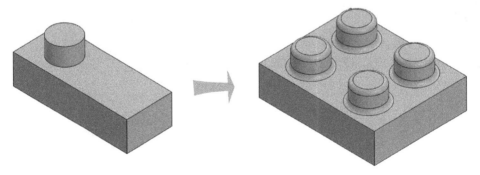

Fig 7-12 Mirror

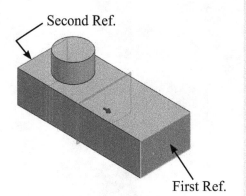

Second Ref.

First Ref.

Fig 7-13 Reference Plane

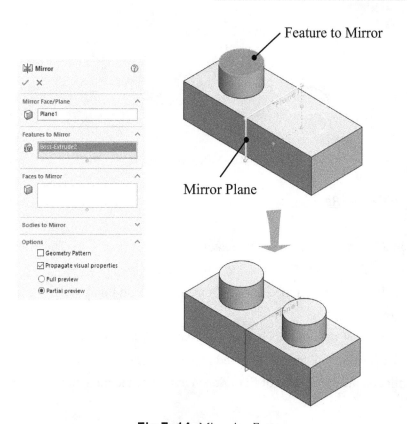

Feature to Mirror

Mirror Plane

Fig 7-14 Mirroring Feature

Mirroring Body

Mirror the body as shown in Fig 7-15.

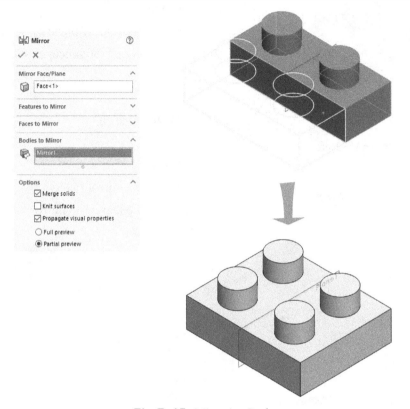

Fig 7-15 Mirroring Body

Adding Fillet and Reordering

1. Apply an R3 mm fillet on the source feature as shown in Fig 7-16. The fillet is registered as the last feature. The fillet is valid only for the source feature.

2. Drag the fillet feature after the Plane1 feature as shown in Fig 7-17. The fillet is valid for the mirrored body.

3. Select the Mirror1 feature and choose Edit Feature. Add Fillet1 as the feature to mirror. The fillet is valid both for the mirrored feature and mirrored body.

4. Apply fillet on the upper edge of Extrude2 to complete the modeling as shown in Fig 7-18.

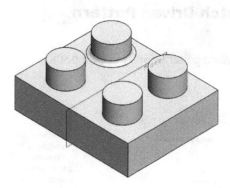

Fig 7-16 Adding Fillet

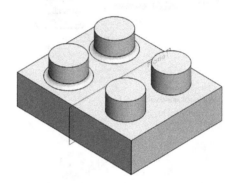

Fig 7-17 Reordering Fillet

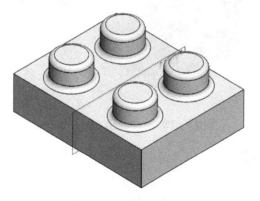

Fig 7-18 Completed Model

7.6 Sketch Driven Pattern

You can create pattern on the sketch points.

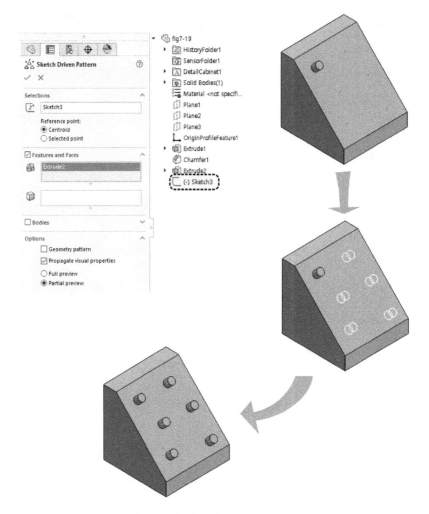

Fig 7-19 Sketch Driven Pattern

Open the given part and complete the modeling by referencing Fig 7-21.

Hints

1. Apply linear pattern once for feature **A**.
2. Apply linear pattern twice for feature **B**.

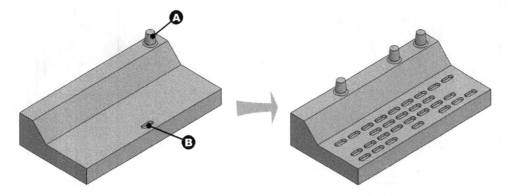

Fig 7-20 Patterned Features

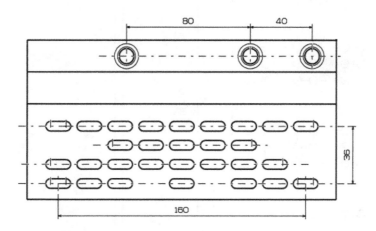

Fig 7-21 Patterned Features

END of Exercise

Exercise 05 — Linear Pattern

ch07_005.SLDPRT

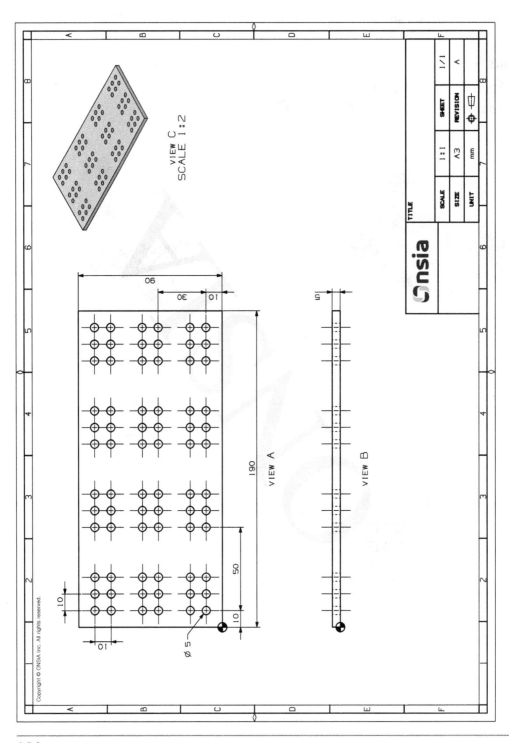

Fig 7-22 Drawing for Exercise 05

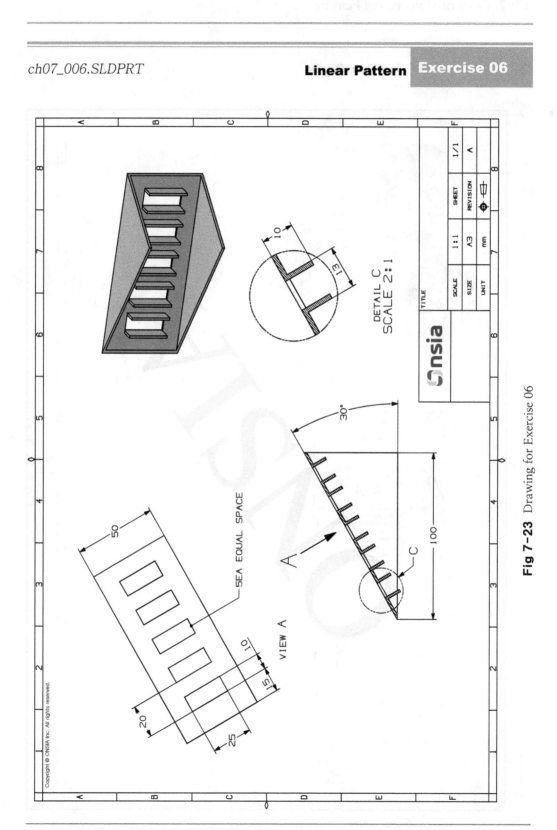

Fig 7-23 Drawing for Exercise 06

DETAIL C
SCALE 2:1

VIEW A

5EA EQUAL SPACE

	SCALE	1:1	SHEET	1/1
	SIZE	A3	REVISION	A
	UNIT	mm		

TITLE

Onsia

Exercise 07 Toy Box Cover

ch07_007.SLDPRT

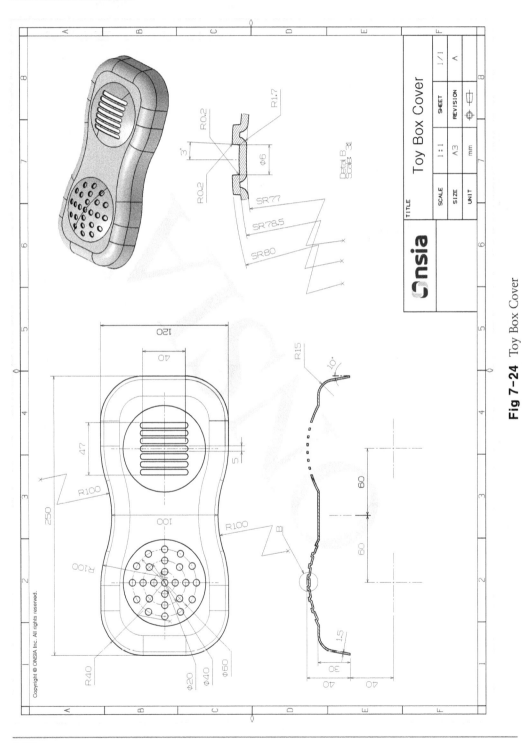

TITLE	Toy Box Cover		
	SCALE 1:1	SHEET 1/1	
	SIZE A3	REVISION A	
	UNIT mm		

Onsia

Fig 7-24 Toy Box Cover

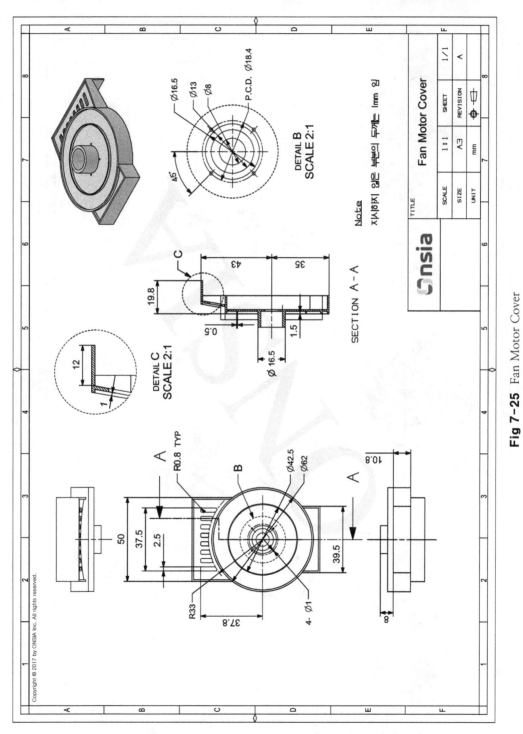

Fig 7-25 Fan Motor Cover

159

Exercise 09   **Lampshade**   *ch07_009.SLDPRT*

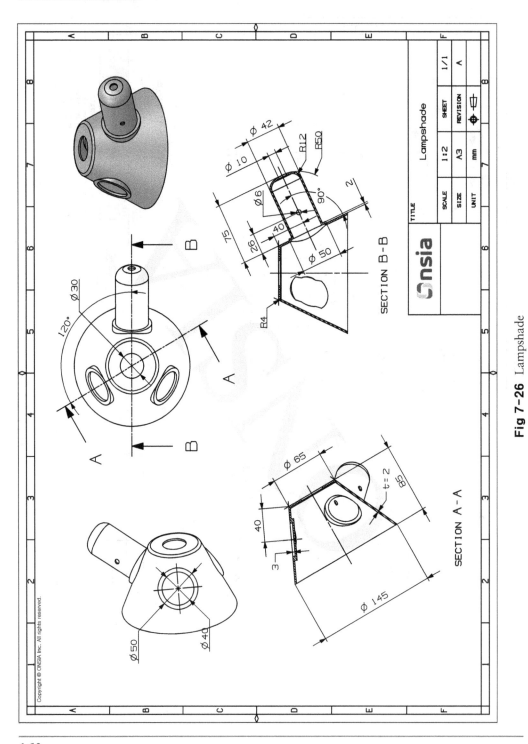

Fig 7-26 Lampshade

160

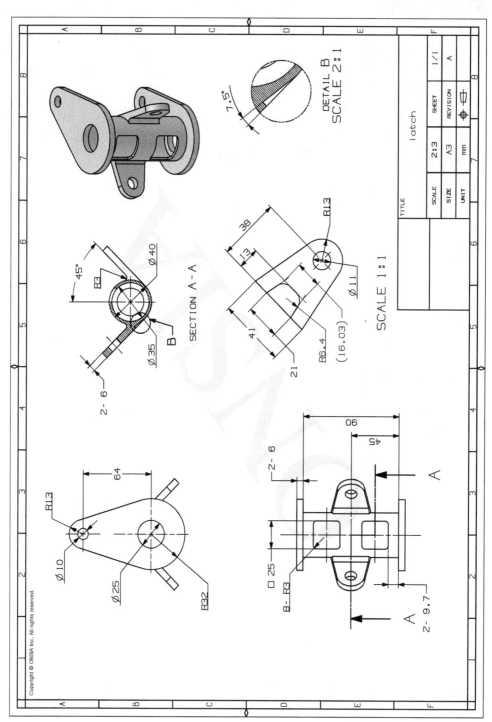

Fig 7-27 Drawing for Exercise 10

Chapter 8
Sweep and Loft

■ After completing this chapter you will understand

- how to create the swept geometries.
- how to create the lofted geometries.

8.1 Sweep

The swept features are created by sweeping a profile along a path.

8.1.1 Swept Boss/Base

This command creates a swept feature. You can use a circular profile or a sketch profile. Note that the profile has to be closed. You can create a hollowed feature by using the Thin Feature option.

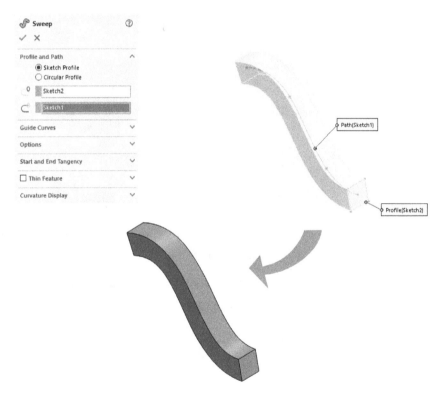

Fig 8-1 Swept Feature Using a Sketch Profile

Let's create a hollowed swept feature along a helix as shown in Fig 8-2.

Fig 8-2 Swept Feature along a Helix

Step 1

1. Create a 60mm diameter circle on the Top plane.

2. Create a counterclockwise helix as shown in Fig 8-3 by using the Helix and Spiral command in the Curves icon group icon the Features tab.

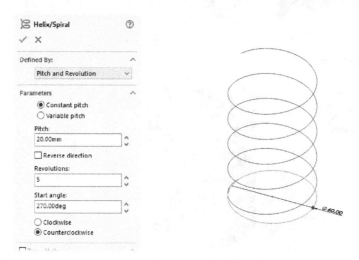

Fig 8-3 Creating a Helix

Step 2

Create a sketch on the Front plane as shown in Fig 8-4. The centroid of the rectangle is at the lower end point of the helix.

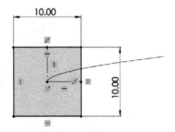

Fig 8-4 Sketch for Profile

Step 3

Create a hollowed swept feature by using the Thin Feature option.

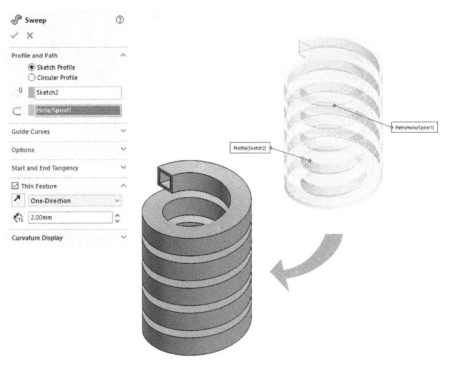

Fig 8-5 Swept Feature

END of Exercise

8.1.2 Swept Surface

You can create a surface without thickness by sweeping an open profile.

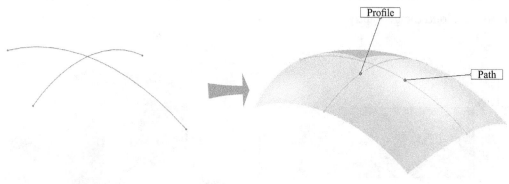

Fig 8-6 Swept Surface

Sweep Surface | Exercise 02

Create a 3D model as shown in Fig 8-7 according to the suggested process..

Fig 8-7 Model to Create

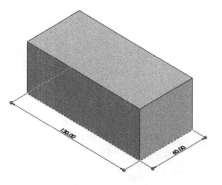

Fig 8-8 Hexahedron

Step 1

Create a 130 x 60 rectangle on the Top plane and extrude it by 50mm. Locate the centroid of the bottom face at the origin.

Step 2

Create an R200 arc for path on the Front plane as shown in Fig 8-9. Locate the center of the arc on the vertical centerline of the hexahedron. Both ends of the arc should be extended beyond the geometry.

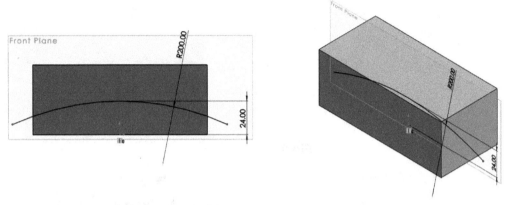

Fig 8-9 Sketch for Path

Step 3

Create an R60 arc for profile on the Right plane as shown in Fig 8-10. Locate the center of the arc on the vertical centerline of the hexahedron. Both ends of the arc should be extended beyond the geometry.

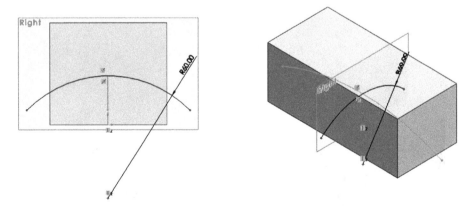

Fig 8-10 Sketch for Profile

Step 4

1. Choose Insert > Surface > Sweep in the SOLIDWORKS menu.

2. Create a swept surface as shown in Fig 8-12 by selecting the profile and path. Choose the Bidirectional option.

Fig 8-11 Surface > Sweep Menu

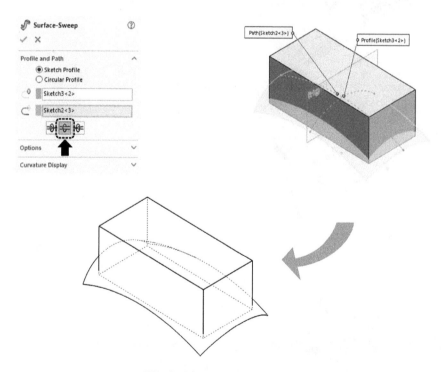

Fig 8-12 Creating Swept Surface

Step 5

1. Choose Insert > Cut > With Surface in the SOLIDWORKS menu.

2. Select the surface.

3. Specify the cut direction upward.

4. Hide the surface.

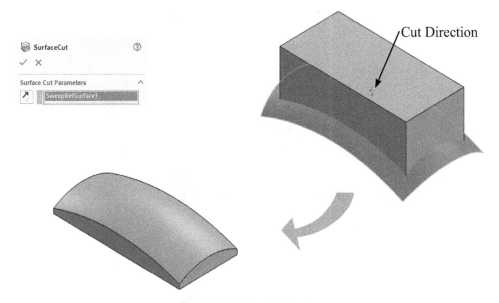

Fig 8-13 Cut with Surface

END of Exercise

8.2 Loft

This command creates a solid body by lofting two or more closed profiles. You can modify the shape by adjusting the connectors and adding guide curves. The Loft command also provides many options such as Start/End Constraints, Close Loft, etc.

8.2.1 Loft Boss/Base

This command creates a lofted feature. All profiles have to be closed. You can use the Thin Feature option to create a hollowed feature.

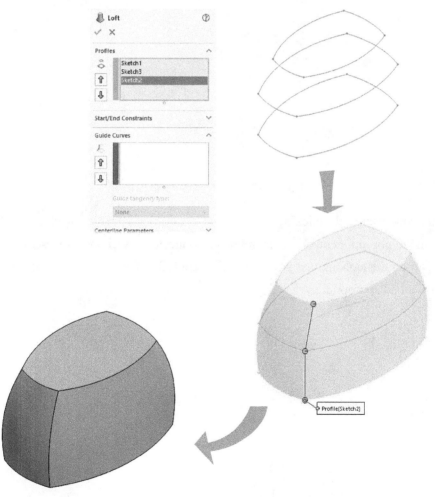

Fig 8-14 Loft Base

8.2.2 Connectors

Connectors specify the connecting points at each profile. If you select two or more profiles, a connector is shown.

To show all connectors, right-click on an empty area in the graphics window and choose Show All Connectors in the pop-up menu. You can adjust the shape of the lofted feature by dragging the connecting points.

Fig 8-15 All Connectors Shown

To add a connector, right-clicking on a specific location on a profile and choose Add Connector in the pop-up menu. You can reset the connectors by choosing Reset Connectors in the pop-up menu. Note that you cannot create a lofted feature if the connecting points are not defined appropriately.

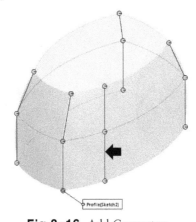

Fig 8-16 Add Connector

Open the given part and create a lofted part as shown in Fig 8-17.

Hint

Add a connector and drag the connecting points.

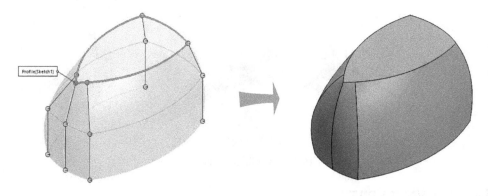

Fig 8-17 Lofted Part

END of Exercise

8.2.3 Guide Curves

With the connectors, you can adjust the location of the connecting points of each profile. The shape of the lofted face is determined by the location and number of the connecting points.

By using guide curves, you can control the shape of the lofted face with a lot of freedom. If the guide curves intersect with profiles, the lofted face satisfies the profiles and guide curves precisely. If the guide curves do not intersect with profiles, the guide curves control the shape of the lofted face out of the lofted face.

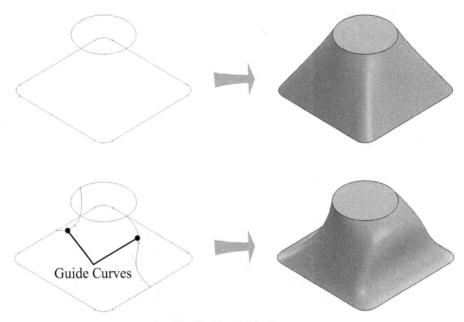

Fig 8-18 Guide Curves

8.2.4 Start/End Constraints

You can specify the forming direction of the lofted face at the start and/or the end profile. It can be normal to profile, or you can specify a direction vector. Fig 8-19 shows the result by specifying Normal to Profile for both the start and end profiles.

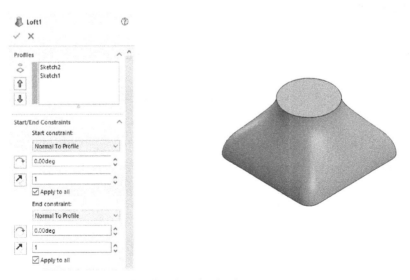

Fig 8-19 Start/End Constraints

8.2.5 Centerline Parameter

You can control the overall shape of the lofted feature by using a centerline. You can use this option in combination with the guide curves.

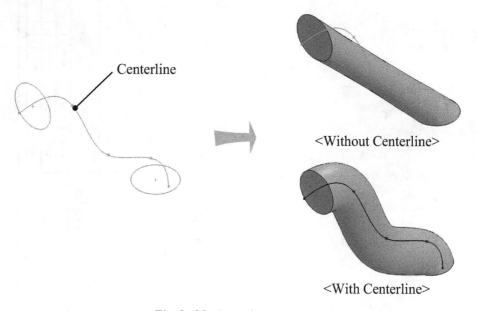

Fig 8-20 Centerline Parameter

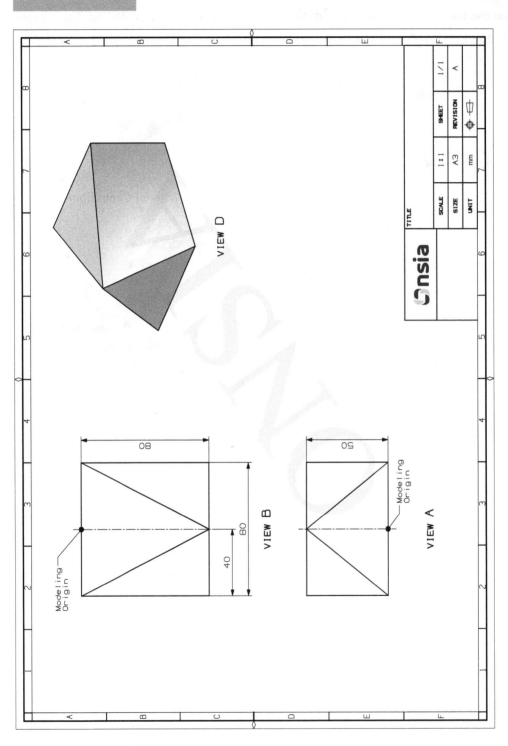

Fig 8-21 Drawing for Exercise 04

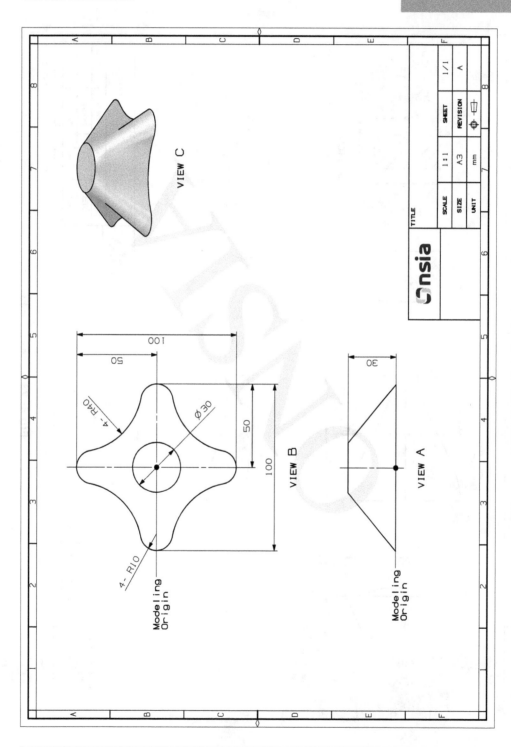

Fig 8-22 Drawing for Exercise 05

Exercise 06   *ch08_006.SLDPRT*

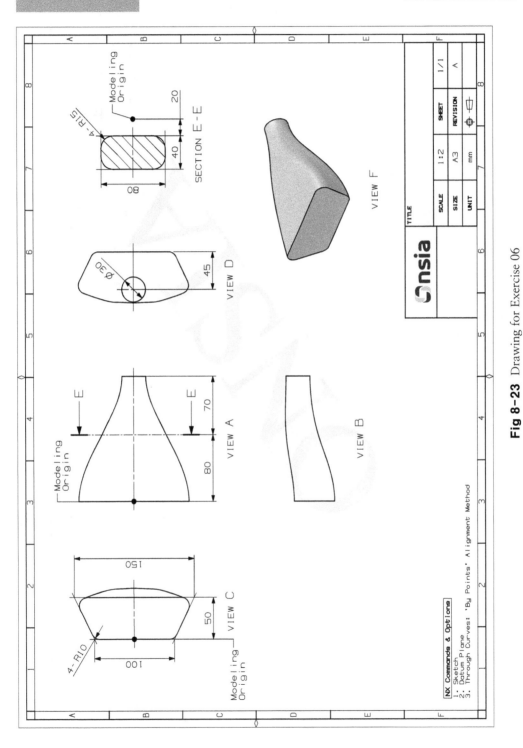

Fig 8-23 Drawing for Exercise 06

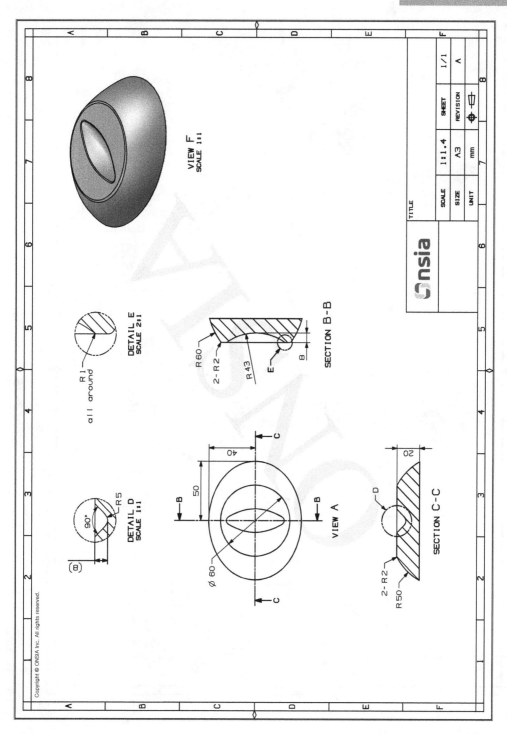

Fig 8-24 Drawing for Exercise 07

ch08_008.SLDPRT

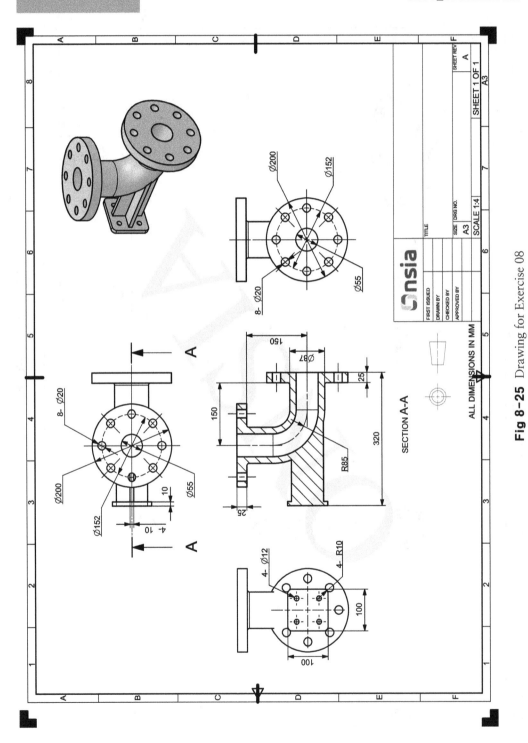

Fig 8-25 Drawing for Exercise 08

Chapter 9
Assembly Design I (Bottom-Up Assembly)

■ After completing this chapter you will understand

- the necessity of assembly design.

- how to construct an assembly.

- how to move or rotate a component.

- how to mate components.

9.1 Introduction

Products we use every day are in an assembled form. After completing the part design, the parts will be manufactured in real life and then assembled so that they function as intended as a complete product. The products will undergo testing if required and then be sold to customers if they pass the tests.

Suppose that we are manufacturing individual parts just after completing the design. If there are problems in the actual assembly, it will take a lot of time, effort and money to correct the design mistakes.

On the other hand, we can replicate assembly on the computer for every part that constitutes the product. We can check interferences, the mechanism and basic physical characteristics such as weight, center of mass, etc. by using the tools in the Assembly tab. If design mistakes are found during the checking process, we can edit the part within the assembly context.

9.2 Terms and Definitions

9.2.1 Bottom-Up Assembly Design

Bottom-Up assembly design refers to an assembly process starting from the bottom of the assembly structure to construct the top assembly. Looking at Fig 9-1, parts A through F are designed in advance independently and assembled to construct sub-assemblies, and finally to construct the top assembly.

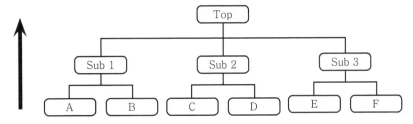

Fig 9-1 Concept Diagram of Bottom-Up Assembly Design

9.2.2 Top-Down Assembly Design

The process of creating certain parts in the context of an assembly is called a top-down assembly design. Referring to the diagram shown in Fig 9-2, the top assembly is constructed with the parts A, B, C, E and F and then the missing part D is created by making the master part a work part. You can also modify a part in the context of an assembly.

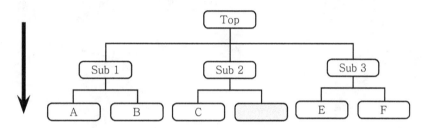

Fig 9-2 Concept Diagram of Top-Down Assembly Design

9.2.3 Part

A part, in general, refers to a single volume solid geometry. We have learned how to create parts in previous chapters. The construction method is saved in the SLDPRT file as the form of features.

9.2.4 Component

If parts are assembled in an assembly, they are called components. Parts used as components do not contain information that defines the part geometry. Instead, the part components only show the resulting geometry and have their own independent appearance, position and orientation.

9.2.5 Sub-assembly

Sub-assembly is a general term to refer to an assembly that is used as a component.

9.3 Constructing an Assembly

In most cases constructing an assembly entails assembling components in the bottom-up assembly design. We will move or constrain the components to define their position and orientation.

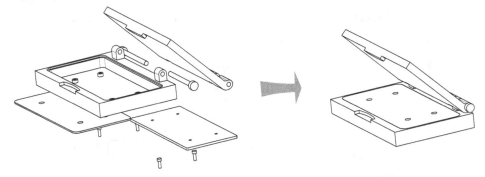

Fig 9-3 Constructing an Assembly

9.3.1 Adding Component

Choose File > New in the Solidworks menu. Choose Assembly in the New Document dialog box and click OK. The New dialog box appears as shown in Fig 9-4. Select the components to add in the assembly and press the Open button.

The preview of the component is displayed as shown in Fig 9-5. You can add the component by clicking the left mouse button. Then the next component is previewed.

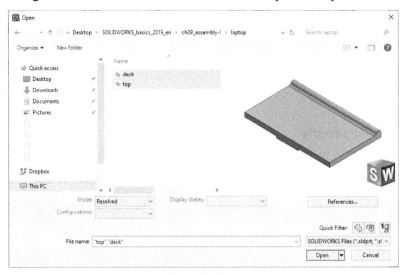

Fig 9-4 Selecting Component

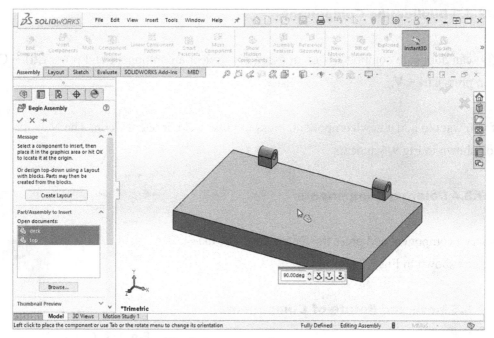

Fig 9-5 Preview of Component

The components are displayed in the assembly design tree as shown in Fig 9-6. The (f) symbol in front of the component name means that the component is fixed. The (-) symbol means that the component is under-defined. The (+) symbol means that the component is over-defined.

Fig 9-6 Assembly Design Tree

9.3.2 Key Functions of Assembly Design

Key functions that are available in Assembly are as follows.

① Creating an Assembly Structure: You can create an assembly using components and/or sub-assemblies.

② Constraining: Define the position and orientation of each component.

③ Interference Detection: Investigate whether the volume of an instance intrudes on other components.

④ Part Modeling: You can create a part referencing the geometry of other components.

⑤ Creating a Disassembled Status: You can disassemble an assembly to create an exploded assembly drawing.

9.3.3 Duplicating Components

You can duplicate components in an assembly. Select a component and press Ctrl + C, then press Ctrl + V.

If you want to add a new component, press the Insert Components icon. The New dialog box shown in Fig 9-4 appears.

9.3.4 Deleting Components

Select a component and press the Delete key. The dialog box shown in Fig 9-7 appears.

Fig 9-7 Confirm Delete

9.3.5 Move and Rotate of Components

You can move or rotate components along the unconstrained direction. This function is useful when you disperse components before mating or for checking constraint status.

Instant Dragging

You can move a component by left-clicking on the component and dragging. You can rotate a component by right-clicking and dragging.

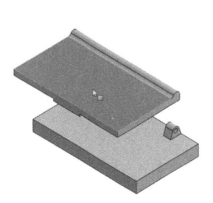

Fig 9-8 Move

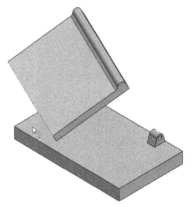

Fig 9-9 Rotate

Using Triad

Right-click on a component and choose "Move with Triad" in the pop-up menu. You can move by left-clicking the arrow and dragging. You can rotate by left-clicking the arc or circle and dragging.

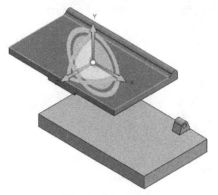

Fig 9-10 Triad

9.4 Mating

You can constrain components' translational or rotational degree of freedom by using the Mate command.

9.4.1 Guidelines for Mating

1. Mate with respect to the fixed or fully defined components.
2. Fully define a component with respect to only one opposite component.
3. Refrain from the closed-loop constraining network as shown in Fig 9-11.

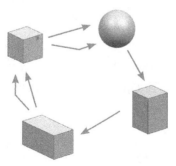

Fig 9-11 Constraining Network(Closed Loop)

9.4.2 Fix

The first added component in an assembly is fixed automatically. If you want to free the fixed component, right-click on the component and choose "Float" in the pop-up menu. To fix a component, choose "Fix" in the pop-up menu. Note that a component is fully defined with respect to a fixed or other fully defined components.

Fig 9-12 "Float" Menu

9.4.3 Mate

Click the Mate icon in the Command Manager. The Mate property manager is invoked as shown in Fig 9-13. If you select elements to apply a mating condition, the component moves to cope with the default condition. You can apply the default mating condition or choose another condition. You can flip the mating direction by pressing the "Flip Mate Alignment" button.

You can apply the mating condition without pressing the Mate icon. Press Ctrl key and select elements in components. The quick tool is available as shown in Fig 9-14, and you can apply the desired mating condition.

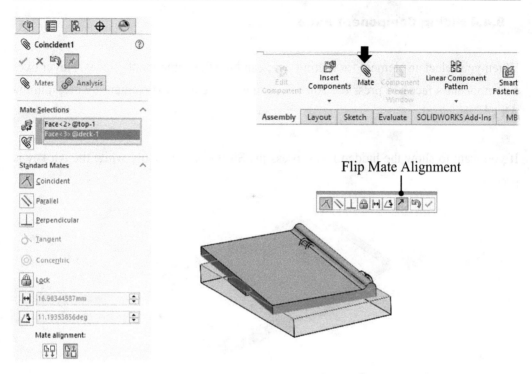

Fig 9-13 Mate Icon and Property Manager

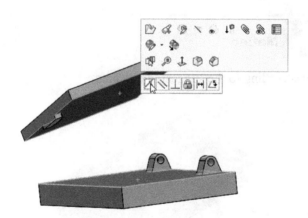

Fig 9-14 Quick Mate

9.4.4 Hiding Component Face

When you select an element for mating, you can hide the components' faces. Hover over a component's face and press the Alt key. You can hide the next element by pressing the Alt key repeatedly.

If you want to show the hidden faces, press the Shift key repeatedly while the Alt key is pressed.

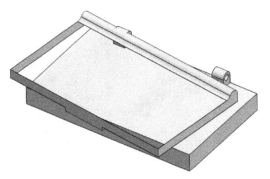

Fig 9-15 Hiding Components' Faces

Exercise 01   **Mating**   *ch09_001.SLDASM*

Mate an assembly according to the suggested procedure.

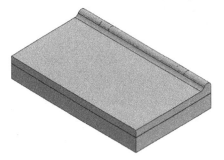

Fig 9-16 Assembly

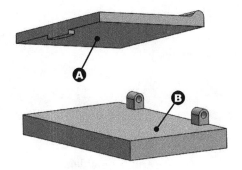

Fig 9-17 Selecting Faces

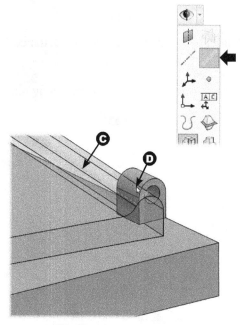

Fig 9-18 Mating Axes

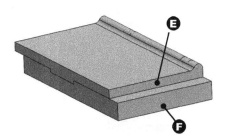

Fig 9-19 Mating Faces

Open Given Part

1. Open the given part (ch09_001.SLD-ASM).

2. Confirm that the deck component is fixed.

Concentric or Coincident

You can apply concentric mating by selecting two cylindrical faces. You can apply coincident mating between two axes of the cylindrical faces by turning on the "View Temporary Axes" button as designated by the arrow in Fig 9-18. In this exercise, take the latter method.

Mating Faces

1. Click the Mate icon.

2. Select the two faces **A** and **B** as shown in Fig 9-17.

3. Confirm that the two faces are aligned and press OK. Note that the Coincident mating is the default when you select two planar faces.

4. Apply the Coincident mating by selecting two faces **E** and **F** as shown in Fig 9-19.

9.4.5 Standard Mate by Entity

The following table lists the valid mates for geometry types.

Mate Element 1	Mate Element 2	Valid Mate Types
Circular or Arc Edge	Cone	Coincident, Concentric
	Cylinder	Concentric, Coincident
	Line	Concentric
	Plane	Coincident
Cone	Cone	Angle, Coincident, Concentric, Distance, Parallel, Perpendicular
	Cylinder	Angle, Concentric, Parallel, Perpendicular
	Plane	Tangent
Cylinder	Circular Edge	Concentric, Coincident
	Cylinder	Angle, Concentric, Distance, Parallel, Perpendicular, Tangent
	Extrusion	Angle, Parallel, Perpendicular, Tangent
	Plane	Distance, Tangent
	Point	Coincident, Concentric, Distance
Extrusion	Cone	Angle, Parallel, Perpendicular
	Extrusion	Angle, Parallel, Perpendicular
	Plane	Tangent
	Point	Coincident
Plane	Circular Edge	Coincident
	Point	Coincident, Distance
	Plane	Angle, Coincident, Distance, Parallel, Perpendicular
	Surface	Tangent

9.4.6 Parent/Child Relationships

Right-click on a component or mating in the assembly design tree and choose Parent/Child in the pop-up menu. Parent/Child relationships are displayed as shown in Fig 9-20.

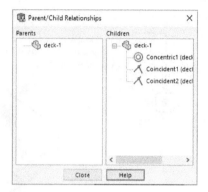

Fig 9-20 Parent/Child Relationships

9.4.7 Suppressing Mating

Right-click on a mating item in the assembly design tree and choose Suppress in the top pop-up menu. The mating condition is deactivated. You can unsuppress the mating by choosing Unsuppress in the pop-up menu.

9.4.8 Showing Mating

Move the mouse pointer on the mating item in the assembly design tree. The mated entities are highlighted as shown in Fig 9-21.

Fig 9-21 Showing Mating

Select several components, right-click, and choose "View Mate" in the pop-up menu. The View Mates window is displayed as shown in Fig 9-22. If you move the mouse cursor on a mating item, the corresponding mating condition is highlighted in the model. You can access the pop-up menu by selecting a mating item in the View Mates window.

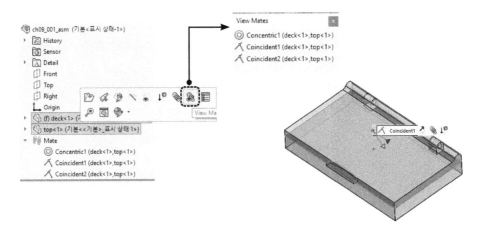

Fig 9-22 View Mate

9.4.9 Smart Mate

Press the Alt key, select a mating entity in a component, and drag the component. The mating condition is snapped and you can apply a mating condition by releasing the mouse left button.

9.4.10 Copy with Mates

Right-click on a component in the assembly design tree and choose "Copy with Mates". Press the "Next" button and select the mating condition to be applied while copying a component.

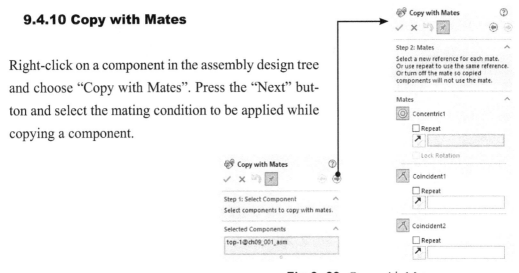

Fig 9-23 Copy with Mates

9.4.11 Width Mate

By using the "Width" in the advanced mates, you can align centers of geometrical entities. Select Face 1 and Face 2 in the Width selections and Face 3 and Face 4 in the Tab selections. You can select a cylindrical face or a reference axis in the Tab selections. The center of Face 1 and Face 2 is aligned with the center of Face 3 and Face 4, cylindrical axis or a reference axis, respectively.

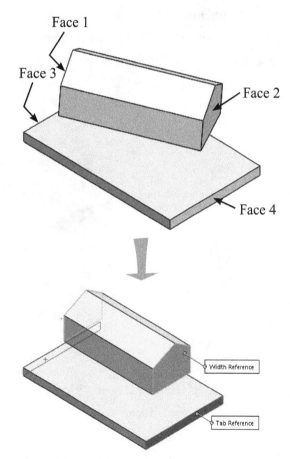

Fig 9-24 Width Mate

Create a Plummer Block assembly by using the given parts in the given folder according to the suggested steps.

Step 1

Create the Plummer Block assembly as shown in Fig 9-25. The Cap and Body faces are mated as designated by **Ⓐ**. Apply Concentric between the cylindrical faces of Brass_Upper and Cap. Apply Concentric between Brass_Lower and Body. The two brasses are overlapped as designated by **Ⓑ**.

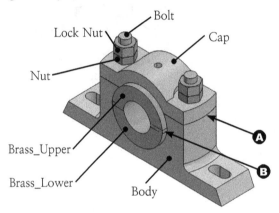

Fig 9-25 Wrong Assembly

Step 2

1. Right-click on Cap and choose "View Mates" and identify the Coincident mate between Cap and Body.

2. Suppress the suspect mate and make it sure by dragging the Cap component.

3. Delete the suspect mate and apply Coincident mate between the axis of brass and the axis of the inner cylindrical axis of Cap.

4. Modify other mates if required.

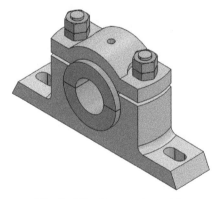

Fig 9-26 Correct Assembly

END of Exercise

Create a Laptop assembly by using the given parts in the ch09_003 folder. Apply 30° open angle for component no.5.

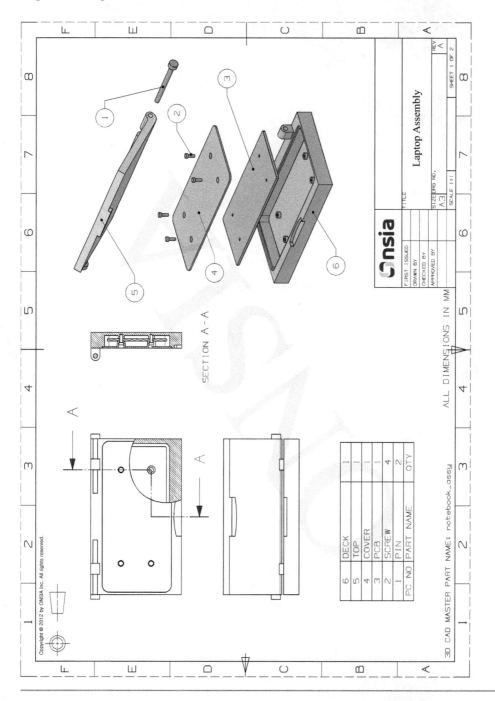

Fig 9-27 Laptop Assembly

This page left blank intentionally.

Chapter 10
Assembly Design II (Top-Down Assembly)

■ After completing this chapter you will understand

- how to edit parts in context of assembly.
- how to detect interference.
- how to create a new part within an assembly.
- how to create a sub-assembly.

10.1 Editing Part

Top-Down assembly design is a concept that you can edit a part in the context of an assembly. To edit a component part in an assembly, select the component in the design tree and click the Edit Component icon in the command manager. You can choose "Edit Part" in the pop-up menu by selecting the component. Or, you can edit features by expanding the modeling history of a part. Note that the assembly is displayed in the graphics window and that other components than being edited are displayed transparently. To finish editing a component, turn off the Edit Component button in the command manager.

If you want to open a component part while you are doing an assembly, select the part and choose "Open Part" in the pop-up menu. To display an assembly again, select the assembly in the SOLIDWORKS menu > Window.

When you are doing a Top-Down design, you have to be well aware of what you are doing in which part. The work part is highlighted in blue and the Features, and Sketch command managers are activated.

Fig 10-1 Edit Component Icon

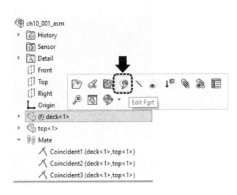

Fig 10-2 Edit Part Menu

Open the given assembly file and edit the erroneous region of the components.

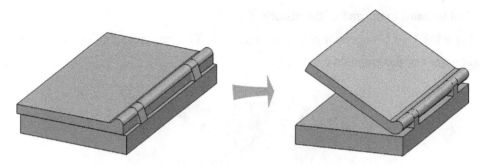

Fig 10-3 Before and After Editing

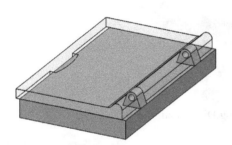

Fig 10-4 Working with the Deck Part

Fig 10-5 Design Tree

Editing a Component

1. Open the ch10_001_asm.SLDASM file in the given folder ch10_001.
2. Examine the shape of the hinge feature of the Deck component. We should edit the Deck component to correct the feature.
3. Select the Deck component in the assembly design tree.
4. Press the Edit Component icon in the command manager.

Design Tree

1. Make sure that the Deck component turns to blue in the design tree.
2. Expand the Deck component.
3. Drag the rollback bar after Extrude2 as shown in Fig 10-5.

Editing Sketch

1. Select Sketch2 of Extrude2 in the design tree.

2. Modify the angle 70° to 90°. Confirm that the geometry is updated.

3. Roll forward to the end of the history.

4. Press the Edit Component button to release it. You can press the icon on the upper right corner of the graphics window.

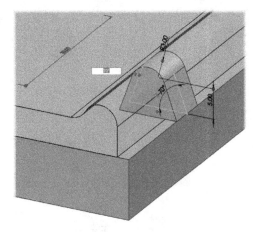

Fig 10-6 Editing Dimension

Editing Assembly Configuration

1. Expand the Mate items in the design tree and suppress the mating that closes the Top component.

2. Right-click the Top component in the design tree and choose Move.

3. Choose "Collision Detection" in the Move Component property manager and drag the Top component by left-clicking. Collision is detected by blue.

4. Press OK to end the Move Component command.

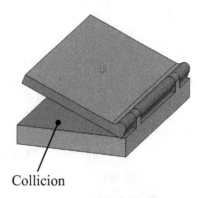

Collicion

Fig 10-7 Collision Detection

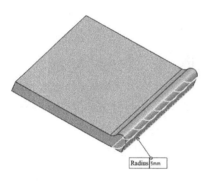

Radius 5mm

Fig 10-8 Adding Fillet

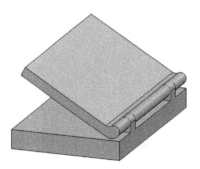

Fig 10-9 Angle

Additional Editing

To avoid a collision while opening the Top component, we need to apply fillet.

1. Change the Top component into the editing mode.
2. Right-click on the Top component and choose "Isolate" in the pop-up menu.
3. Apply an R5 mm fillet as shown in Fig 10-8.
4. Press the "Exit Isolate" button.
5. Exit the editing mode.
6. Apply a 30° opening angle to the Top component.

END of Exercise

10.2 Save As

To maintain the older version of an assembly part after editing, you need to use the Save As command. Enter the revised name of an assembly in the Save As dialog box as shown in Fig 10-10. Choose an option in **Ⓐ**.

- Save As: The older assembly file is closed without saving, and the new file is open.
- Save as Copy and continue: The older assembly file is open, and the edited file is closed with being saved as a designated name.
- Save as copy and open: The older assembly file is loaded without saving, and the new file is open as a work part.

With option **Ⓑ** in Fig 10-10, you can save as the components with a prefix or suffix.

With the advanced option **Ⓒ**, you can designate individual names for each component part. By clicking the region **Ⓓ** in Fig 10-11, you can edit the name of components. By double-clicking the region **Ⓔ** in Fig 10-11, you can change the path of the component files.

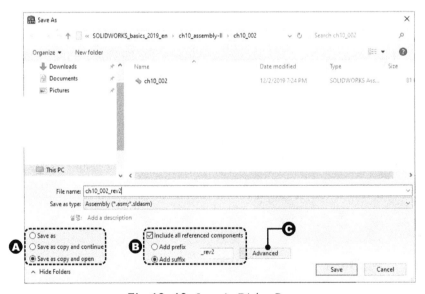

Fig 10-10 Save As Dialog Box

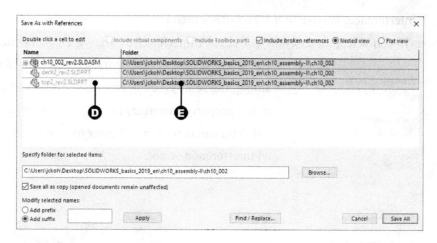

Fig 10-11 Advanced Option

10.3 Interference Detection

The purpose of assembling parts on a computer is to check for design errors before manufacturing the parts. The fundamental issue arising in checking an assembly is interference. We first assemble parts according to their design position and orientation and then check if the geometry of the part intrudes on the volume of another part.

Component 1 in Fig 10-12 has a hole diameter φ30 which is smaller than the outer diameter φ35 of Component 2. Therefore, we cannot assemble Component 2 into the hole of Component 1 using actual parts. However, using 3D modeling software such as SOLIDWORKS, we can assemble Component 1 and 2 irrespective of their sizes. Therefore, after assembling the components in their correct position, we need to check if they interfere with each other.

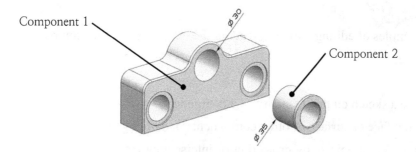

Fig 10-12 Assembly with Interference

To check interference, choose SOLIDWORKS menu > Tools > Evaluate > Interference Detection. If you select an assembly, it checks interferences among all components. If

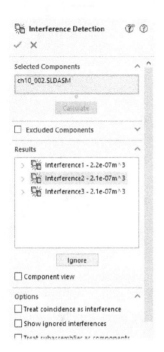

you select several components, it checks interferences among the selected components. If you select a result in the property manager, the region is highlighted in red. You can determine whether to modify the detected interference or not.

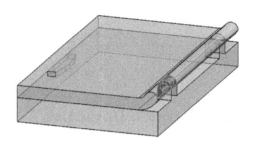

Fig 10-13 Collision Detection

10.4 Modifying Parts in the Context of Assembly

After checking for interference, we have to edit the parts if any undesired interference is detected between the components. When we modify the parts, it would be convenient if we could make reference to the geometry of the other components that will be assembled with the interested parts. This method of part modeling or editing is available if we turn a component into an edit mode.

Typical examples of editing parts referencing the geometry of other components include the following.

① Create a sketch on the geometry of a component.
② Use the face or surface of other components in defining an extrude feature.
③ Create sketch objects by projecting or intersecting the geometry of other components.

In this exercise we will perform;

1. Interference Detection
2. Editing Part
3. Saving as New Part

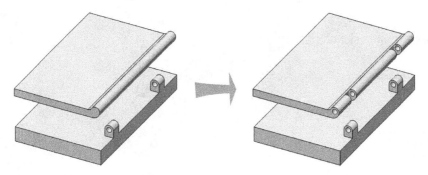

Fig 10-14 Before and After Editing

Interference Detection

1. Open the given part.
2. Choose SOLIDWORKS menu > Tools > Evaluate > Interference Detection.
3. Make sure that the assembly is selected and press the Calculate button.
4. Review the three interferences one by one by clicking in the Results window.
5. Press OK to finish.

We need to modify each interference. To avoid interference 1, we need to modify the Deck component. To avoid interference 2 and 3, we need to modify the Top component.

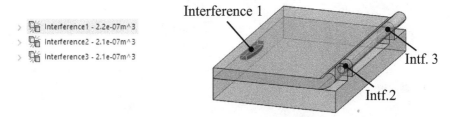

Fig 10-15 Interference Detection

Modifying Intf. 2 and 3

We will remove the Top component to avoid interference.

1. Make the Top component an edit mode.
2. Define a sketch on the upper face. (**A** in Fig 10-16)
3. Click the Convert Entities icon, select six edges as designated in Fig 10-16 and press OK.
4. Close the open sketch by line.

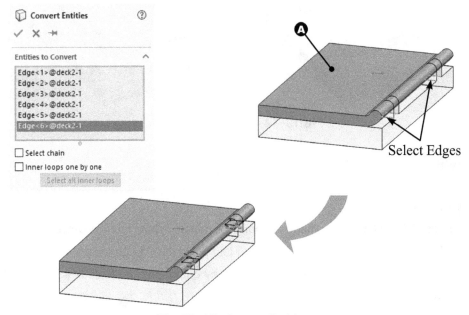

Fig 10-16 Convert Entities

Fig 10-17 Top Component Modified

5. Exit the sketch and cut by extruding the sketch. Choose Through All - Both as Direction 1.
6. Finish the edit mode.

Modifying Intf.1

We will modify the Deck component to avoid interference.

1. Make the Deck component an edit mode.
2. Hide the Top component and define a sketch on the upper face of Deck.
3. Click the Convert Entities icon and select the face as designate in Fig 10-18.
4. Exit the sketch and cut by extruding the sketch. Choose Up to Surface as the Direction 1 option and select the bottom face of the extruded feature of the Top component.
5. Finish the edit mode.

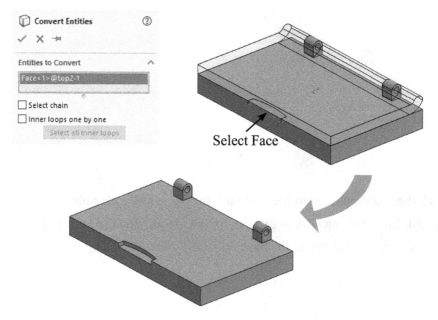

Fig 10-18 Modifying Deck Component

Save As

We will save the deck2 and top2 components as deck2_rev2 and top2_rev2, respectively. The assembly file will be saved as ch10_002_rev2, and the old assembly with the older version of components will be open.

1. Choose File > Save As in the SOLIDWORKS menu.

2. Enter "_rev2" behind the assembly file name.

3. Choose "Save as copy and open" option in the Save As dialog box.

4. Choose "Include all referenced components" option and add suffix "_rev2".

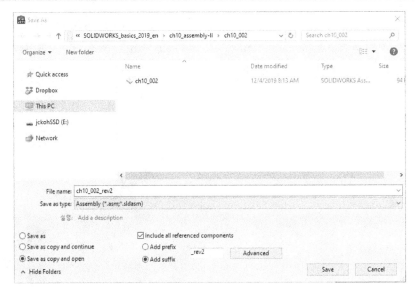

Fig 10-19 Save As

5. Click the "Advanced" button and modify the name of the assembly file as shown in Fig 10-20. Note that you have to press Enter after modifying the assembly file name.

6. Press the Save All button in the Save As with References dialog box.

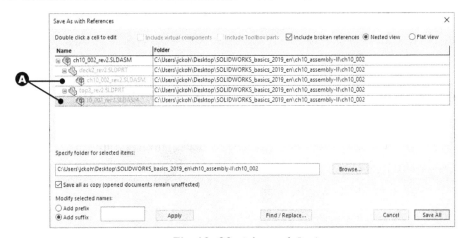

Fig 10-20 Advanced Option

You can display the location of the reference files, as shown in Fig 10-21, by choosing File > Find Reverences in the SOLIDWORKS menu. Note that the referenced modification will not be updated if the reference files are not found.

Fig 10-21 Find References

7. Close the older assembly file without saving.

8. Open the two assembly files and verify the modification status of the components. The older assembly file ch10_002 should have the older components, and the newer assembly file ch10_002_rev2 should have the renamed components.

END of Exercise

Parent/Child Relationships

If you modify a component by referencing other components, the parent/child relationships are established. If the parent geometry is changed, the child geometry is updated.

The parent/child relationships are affected by the location and orientation of components. Therefore, you should not move or rotate components if you have modified a component with links.

If you want to break all relationships, right-click on assembly and choose External References in the pop-up menu. Press Break All in the dialog box. You can break individual relationship by right-clicking on a feature.

10.5 Adding New Part

If you want to insert an existing part, use the Insert Component icon. If you are going to add a new component, use the New Part icon. You can create geometry in the new component by entering the edit mode.

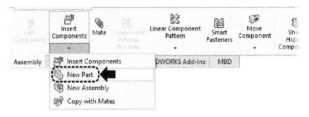

Fig 10-22 New Part Icon

Exercise 03   **Adding New Component**   *Folder: ch010_003*

Open the given assembly and create the pin component.

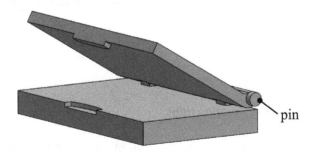

Fig 10-23 Creating Pin Component

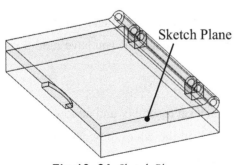

Fig 10-24 Sketch Plane

Adding a Part

1. Open the given assembly file. (ch10_003_asm)

2. Click the New Part icon and select the sketch plane as designated in Fig 10-24. Part1 is inserted with the edit mode.

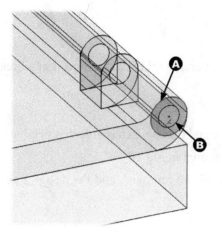

Fig 10-25 Sketch

Creating Pin Geometry

1. Create two circles for head (**A** in Fig 10-25) and for body(**B** in Fig 10-25).
2. Create the pin geometry by extruding 3mm for head and 40mm for body as shown in Fig 10-26.

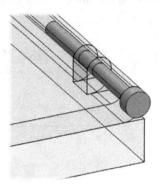

Fig 10-26 Geometry of Pin

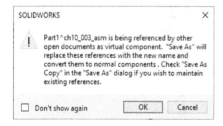

Fig 10-27 Information

Save

1. While you are in the edit mode of Part1, choose File > Save As in the SOLIDWORKS menu.
2. Press OK in the information window as shown in Fig 10-27.
3. Enter pin as the file name and press the Save button in the Save As dialog box.
4. Finish the edit mode.

Breaking Relationships

You cannot move components in case there exist parent/child relationships. Let's break links.

1. Right-click on top assembly in the design tree and choose External References.
2. Press the Break All button in the dialog box shown in Fig 10-28.
3. Press OK in the information box. All references are removed, and the design tree is shown like Fig 10-29.

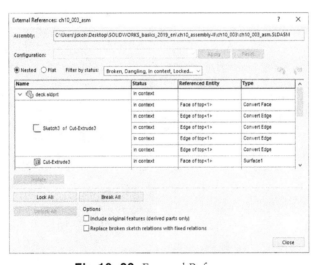

Fig 10-28 External References

<Before Break>   <After Break>

Fig 10-29 Before and After Breaking

Fig 10-30 InPlace Relation

Assembling

1. Note that InPlace relation is established between the Top and Pin components as designated by the arrow in Fig 10-30.
2. Copy the Pin component and assembly on the other side.
3. Open the Top component 30 degree as shown in Fig 10-31.
4. Save the assembly file.

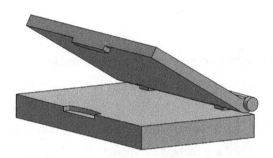

Fig 10-31 Completed Assembly

END of Exercise

 No External References

Press the No External References button in the edit mode for creating component geometry without building external references.

10.6 Sub-Assembly

Sub-assembly is used as a component of another assembly. A sub-assembly in the real world is a product in itself. For example, an engine is a sub-assembly of an automobile assembly. You can construct another sub-assembly in an existing sub-assembly. For example, the cylinder head assembly can be constructed as a sub-assembly of the engine assembly.

You can create a sub-assembly in SOLIDWORKS according to two approach.

- Bottom-Up: Create a Sub-assembly → Add Components → Mate → Save → Add it as a Component of another Assembly
- Top-Down: Create an Assembly → Insert a New Assembly → Add Components in the New Assembly → Mate

In the bottom-up approach, we create and mate a sub-assembly, save the assembly file and construct the upper assembly. Therefore, it takes much time than the top-down approach.

In the top-down approach, the following practice still valid.
- When you are mating components in a sub-assembly, you have to make the sub-assembly an edit mode.
- A fixed component is required to fully define a component through mating.

When you added a sub-assembly several times, components in each sub-assembly must have the same assembly status. For example, the sub-assembly A shown in Fig 10-33 has been added twice. The bushing and support components cannot have different assembly status. If a different location and orientation are required for components, you have to create respective sub-assemblies.

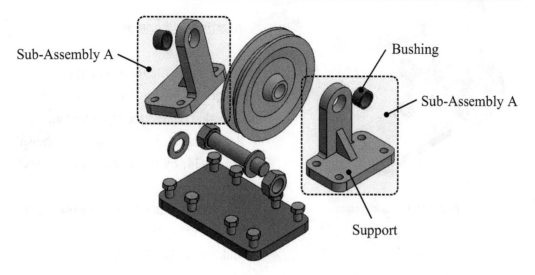

Fig 10-32 Pulley Support Assembly

Sub-Assembly - Top Down   **Exercise 04**

Let's create the Pulley Support assembly as shown in Fig 10-33 with the top down approach.

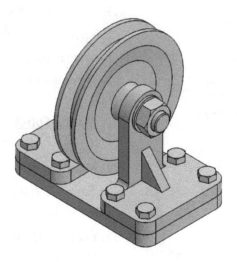

Fig 10-33 Pulley Support Assembly

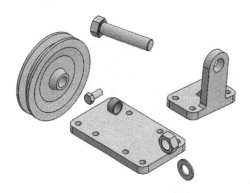

Fig 10-34 Components

Inserting Components

1. Create a new file for assembly.
2. Select all eight parts in the given folder ch10_004 and press the Open button.
3. Rotate the Base component as shown in Fig 10-34, by using the rotate context toolbar.
4. Insert the remaining components as shown in Fig 10-34.
4. Make sure that the Base component is fixed.
5. Save the part file as the name of pulley_support_asm.

pulley_support_asm (Default<Display State-
▸ History
  Sensors
▸ Annotations
  Front Plane
  Top Plane
  Right Plane
  Origin
▸ (f) base<1>
▸ (-) bolt_M12<1>
▸ (-) bushing<1>
▸ (-) Nut<1>
▸ (-) pulley<1>
▸ (-) Shoulder_screw<1>
▸ (-) support<1>
▸ (-) washer<1>
▸ (-) [Assem5^pulley support asm]<1>
  Mates   Move to Assem5^pulley_support_asm-1

Fig 10-35 Drag

Creating Sub-Assembly

1. Choose the New Assembly icon in the Insert Components icon group.
2. Select the Bushing and the Support components in the design tree, drag and drop in the new assembly as shown in Fig 10-35.

Mating Sub-Assembly

1. Make the sub-assembly an edit mode.
2. Save the sub-assembly as the name of support_asm.
3. Fix the Support component.
4. Mate the Bushing component in the hole of support.
5. Save the support component.
6. Finish the edit mode.

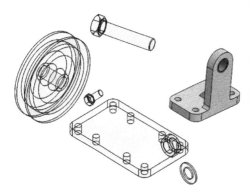

Fig 10-36 Mating Support_asm

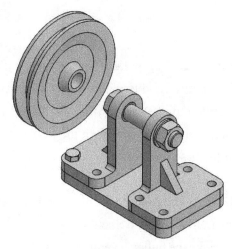

Fig 10-37 Partial Mating

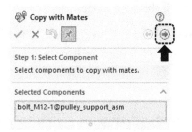

Fig 10-38 Copy with Mates

Mating Top Assembly

1. Copy and paste the support_asm.

2. Mate the sub-assembly and components as shown in Fig 10-37. Note that a bolt_ M12 is mated with Concentric and Coincident conditions and Pulley is not mated.

3. Close the Mate property manager and Right-click on bolt_M12 and choose Copy with Mates in the pop-up menu.

4. Press the Next button in the property manager as designated in Fig 10-38.

5. Select the cylindrical face for the Concentric condition and the planar face for the Coincident condition as designated in Fig 10-39.

6. Repeat the same process to copy bolt_ M12 with mates.

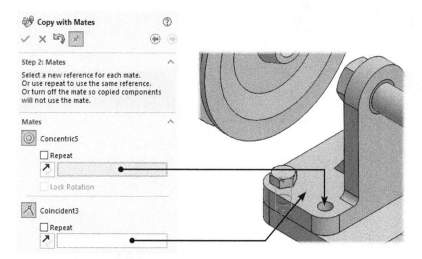

Fig 10-39 Copy and Paste with Mate

Plane

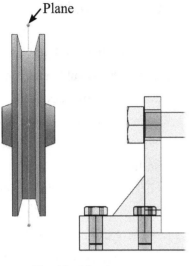

Fig 10-40 Plane

Mating Pulley

For assembling pulley, we first apply the Concentric condition. Then we will create a middle plane as shown in Fig 10-40 to make it be coincident with the right plane of the base component.

1. Apply the concentric condition between the pulley hole and Shoulder screw.
2. Make the pulley an edit mode and create a plane as shown in Fig 10-40.
3. Finish the edit mode.
4. Apply the coincident condition between the plane of pulley and the right plane of base.

Note that you can apply the Width mating instead of applying the coincident mating between planes.

Fig 10-41 shows the completed assembly.

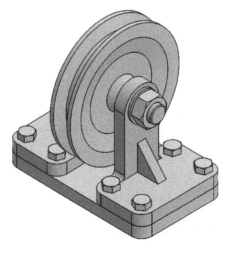

Fig 10-41 Completed

END of Exercise

10.7 Join and Cavity

You can join components into one and remove the common geometry. If you want to join the component B to component A, make the component A an edit mode and choose Insert > Features > Add in the SOLIDWORKS menu. The property of the added geometry is inherited from component A.

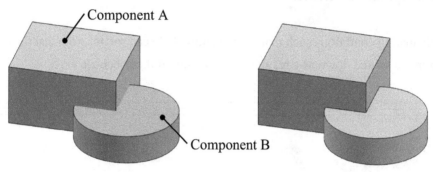

Component A

Component B

Fig 10-42 Join

If you want to remove the component B from component A, make the component A an edit mode and choose Insert > Features > Cavity in the SOLIDWORKS menu. The resulting geometry of the component is as shown in Fig 10-43. Component B is hidden in the figure.

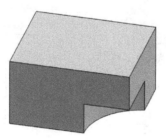

Fig 10-43 Cavity

Exercise 05 **Part Modeling in Assembly** *Folder: ch010_005*

1. Create an assembly as shown in Fig 10-44. Note that the Link component is missing.

2. Create the Link part in the assembled position with appropriate arbitrary dimensions such that there are no interferences.

3. Apply mating conditions such that the Eccentric Axle can rotate. Note that the Connector can move up and down as a result of the rotation of the eccentric axle.

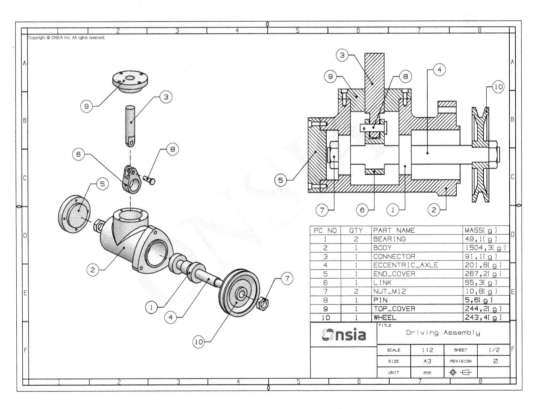

PC NO	QTY	PART NAME	MASS[g]
1	2	BEARING	49,1[g]
2	1	BODY	1504,3[g]
3	1	CONNECTOR	91,1[g]
4	1	ECCENTRIC_AXLE	201,8[g]
5	1	END_COVER	267,2[g]
6	1	LINK	55,3[g]
7	2	NUT_M12	10,8[g]
8	1	PIN	5,6[g]
9	1	TOP_COVER	244,2[g]
10	1	WHEEL	243,4[g]

⌂nsia

TITLE Driving Assembly

SCALE	1:2	SHEET	1/2
SIZE	A3	REVISION	0
UNIT	mm		

Fig 10-44 Driving Assembly

Chapter 11
Drawing

■ After completing this chapter you will understand

- objectives and types of drawings.

- projection methods.

- the process of creating each drawing view in SOLIDWORKS.

- types of various drawing views and how to create them in SOLIDWORKS.

- how to create dimensions and modify their properties.

- how to create an assembly drawing.

11.1 Introduction

A drawing explains the shapes and manufacturing methods of a part or product. We also use a drawing for inspection. These days, three-dimensional design is widely adopted in designing products in manufacturing industries. But, we frequently use drawings for clear communication between the designers and the manufacturers.

There are two types of drawings based on the objectives of drawings; a part drawing and an assembly drawing. A part drawing is created to manufacture individual parts. An assembly drawing is created for assembly. The assembly sequence and path can be illustrated in a disassembled drawing view. Names, quantity, material, etc. of each component of an assembly can be included in the parts list.

In SOLIDWORKS, we can create each drawing view by referencing a three dimensional part geometry. If the part geometry is modified, the drawing can be updated to adapt to the design changes.

The general process to create a drawing is as follows.

① Determine a part or assembly for which to create the drawing.
② Create a drawing file.
③ Create drawing views required to explain the three dimensional shape of the part.
④ Create dimensions, annotations, symbols, etc. in the drawing.

11.2 Terms and Definitions

11.2.1 Drawing View

The three dimensional part geometry can be viewed from various directions or can be cut or magnified to express its shape completely in two dimensions.

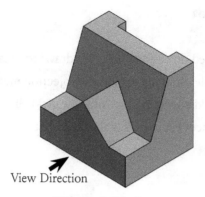

Fig 11-1 3D Geometry

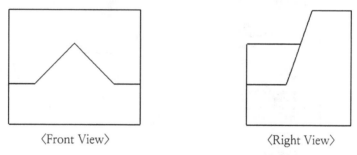

⟨Front View⟩　　　　　　　⟨Right View⟩

Fig 11-2 Drawing Views (3rd Angle Projection)

11.2.2 Title Block

Basic information for a drawing is recorded in the title block which is located in the bottom right of the drawing sheet. Fig 11-3 shows a typical title block that is available by default in SOLIDWORKS

Fig 11-3 Title Block

11.2.3 Drawing Sheet

A manual drawing is created on a sheet. In a 2D drawing created with a CAD program, the size of the drawing, scale, drawing standard, projection method, etc. are defined in the drawing sheet. You can add sheets by pressing the Add Sheet button below the design tree. Fig 11-4 shows the Sheet Properties dialog box that is available by right-clicking on the sheet in the design tree.

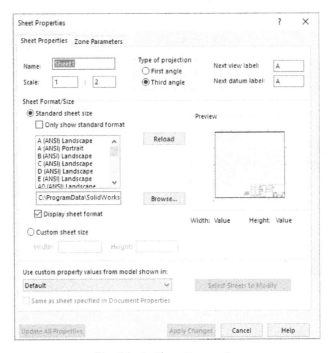

Fig 11-4 Sheet Propertties

11.2.4 Sheet Format/Size

The types of title block and sheet frame are set in the Sheet Format/Size option. You can use a standard sheet size, or you can use your own sheet size by choosing the Custom Sheet Size option.

If you choose a standard sheet size, you can apply a default title block and frame. You can edit the sheet format by right-clicking on a sheet and choosing Edit Sheet Format in the pop-up menu. When you have edited a sheet format or create a new sheet format, you can save the sheet format by choosing File > Save Sheet Format in the SOLIDWORKS menu.

11.2.5 Projection Method

If you misunderstand the projection method, the projected shape on the right and left can be reversed. The same is true for the top and bottom shape. The projection method is specified in the drawing sheet.

1st Angle Projection: A part is placed in the 1st quadrant in the space and is projected on each plane along the projection direction. The plane of projection is unfolded to arrange each projection view as shown in Fig 11-5.

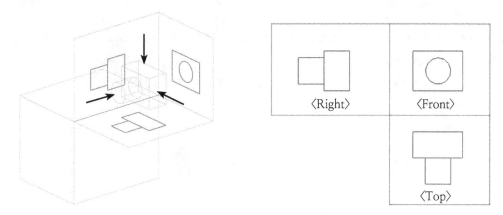

Fig 11-5 1st Angle Projection

3rd Angle Projection: A part is placed in the 3rd quadrant in the space and is projected on each plane along the projection direction. The plane of projection is unfolded to arrange each projection view as shown in Fig 11-6.

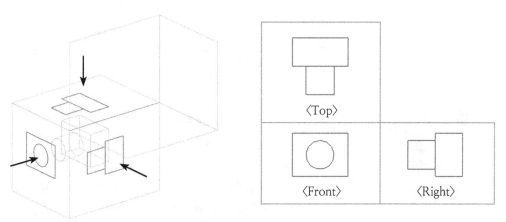

Fig 11-6 3rd Angle Projection

11.3 Drawing File and Projected View

A drawing file in SOLIDWORKS has an extension of *.SLDDRW. In general, 3D model data and its drawings are saved in separate files. When you have modified the 3D geometry in the part file, you can update the drawing file.

Exercise 01	Drawing File, Projected View	ch11_001.SLDPRT

Let's do the following work according to the given process.

1. Create a drawing file and create projected views. Display the hidden lines.
2. Save the file and open it.
3. Edit the 3D geometry in the part file and update the drawing file.

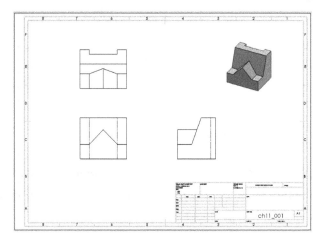

Fig 11-7 Drawing to Create

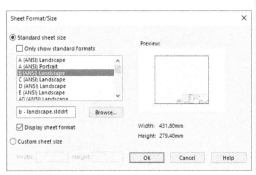

Fig 11-8 Sheet Properties

Creating a New File, Model View and Projected View

1. Create a new drawing part.

2. Set the sheet format as shown in Fig 11-8.

3. Press the Browse button in the Model View property manager and select the part to insert (ch11_001.SLDPRT).

Fig 11-9 Part to Insert   **Fig 11-10** Model View

4. Select Front in the second step and select the Preview option. If you move the mouse pointer on the sheet, the preview is available.

5. Create the Front drawing view as shown in Fig 11-11. The Projected View command is executed automatically.

6. Create the Top and Right drawing view as shown in Fig 11-12.

7. Finish the Projected View command by pressing OK.

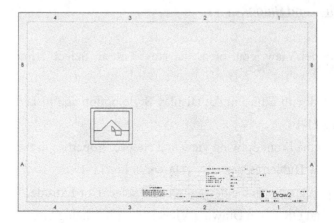

Fig 11-11 Front View

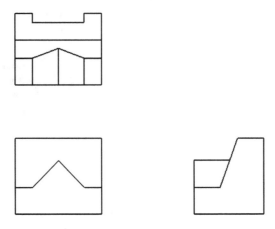

Fig 11-12 Projected View

Scale and Unit

1. Change the unit to MMGS, if not.

2. Change the scale to 2:3 in the sheet property.

3. Drag the drawing views to the appropriate position as shown in Fig 11-14.

Fig 11-13 Scale and Unit

Trimetric View and Hidden Lines

1. Click the Model View icon, press the Next button. Select Trimetric in the More Views option.

2. Choose Shaded with Edges in the Display Style option and place the drawing view as shown in Fig 11-14.

3. Right-click on the Front drawing view and choose Properties in the pop-up menu.

4. Select the Show Hidden Edges tab as shown in Fig 11-15.

5. Expand the part history in the design tree and select Cut-Extrude1.

6. Press Apply and OK in the Drawing View Properties dialog box.

7. Show hidden lines in the two projected views.

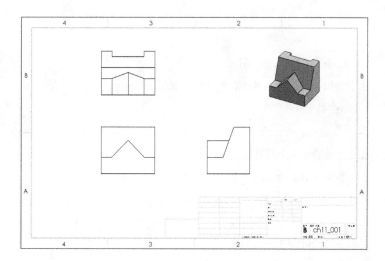

Fig 11-14 Trimetric View

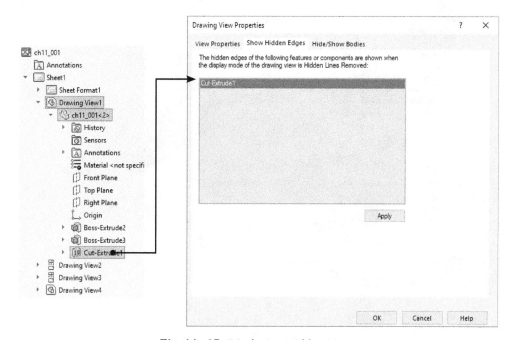

Fig 11-15 Displaying Hidden Lines

Save and Close

1. Choose File > Save in the menu and enter the same name as the part.
2. Choose File > Close.

Edit Part

1. Open the drawing file.

2. Right-click on a drawing view in the design tree and choose Open Part in the pop-up menu.

3. Select the sketch of Cut-Extrude1 and change the dimension **A** to 20.

4. Press the Rebuild button (Ctrl+B).

5. Choose the drawing file in the Menu > Window.

6. Make sure that the drawing views have been updated and close the files.

Proceed to the next exercise.

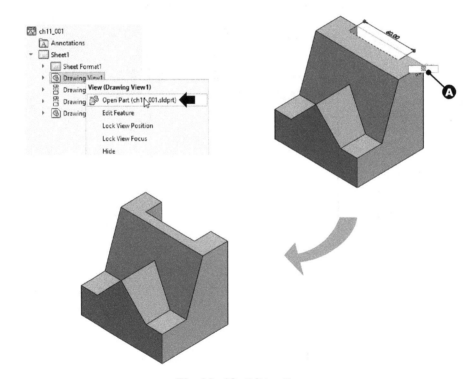

Fig 11-16 Editing Part

END of Exercise

Let's create the title block in a sheet.

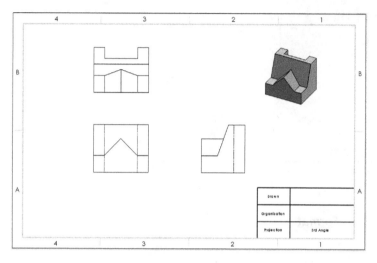

Fig 11-17 Editing Sheet Format

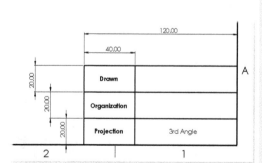

Fig 11-18 New Title Block

Deleting and Creating Title Block

1. Open the drawing file of Exercise01.
2. Right-click on Sheet1 and choose Edit Sheet Format.
3. Delete the existing title block.
4. Draw a title block as shown in Fig 11-18, by using the sketch tools. You can enter texts by using the Note icon in the Annotation tab.
5. Hide all dimensions.
6. Right-click on Sheet1 and choose Edit Sheet. Fig 11-19 shows the edited sheet format.

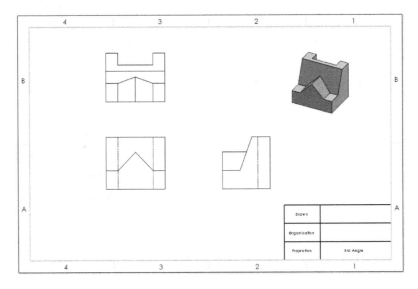

Fig 11-19 Edited Sheet Format

Saving Sheet Format

1. Choose Menu > File > Save Sheet Format.
2. Enter the file name and press Save in the dialog box.

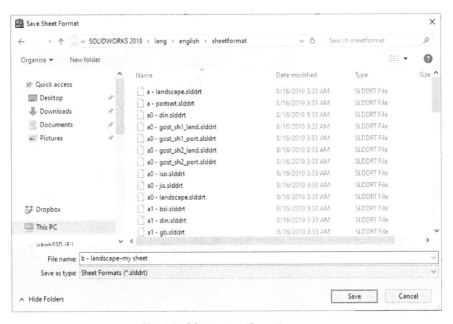

Fig 11-20 Saving Sheet Format

Applying Sheet Format

1. Press the Add Sheet button at the bottom of the design tree.

2. Right-click on Sheet2 and choose Properties.

3. Choose the Standard Size Sheet option and select the sheet format that you have created.

4. Press the Apply Changes button.

Fig 11-21 Applying Sheet Format

11.4 Drawing Views

You can create various drawing views by using the tools in the View Layout command manager.

- Standard 3 Views: Front, Right, Top view are created automatically.
- Model View: Drawing view is created on the basis of the standard part views.
- Projected View: An existing drawing view is projected at a right angle according to the specified projection method.
- Auxiliary View: An existing drawing view is projected a an arbitrary angle according to the specified projection method.
- Section View: An existing drawing view is cut at a location and is viewed along a specified direction. The cut face is hatched.
- Detail View: A complex portion of another view is magnified.
- Broken-out Section View: A portion of an existing view is cut out at a specified depth.
- Broken View: A long uniform part can be cut short.

Fig 11-22 View Layout Tools

11.4.1 Projected View

You can create a projected view according to the following process.

1. Create a parent view.
2. Press the Projected View icon.
3. Select the parent view.
4. Move the mouse to the projection direction and click to specify the position.

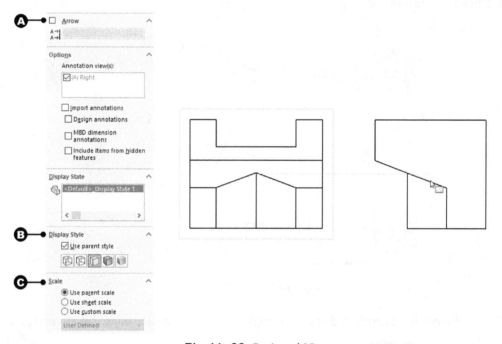

Fig 11-23 Projected View

Ⓐ: You can create a projection arrow.

Ⓑ: You can use the same display style as the parent view or use another style..

Ⓒ: You can use parent scale, sheet scale or custom scale.

11.4.2 Auxiliary View

You can project a parent view other than the right angle or 45 degrees according to the following process.

1. Create a parent view.
2. Click the Auxiliary View icon.
3. Select the reference edge in the parent view.
4. Click the location.

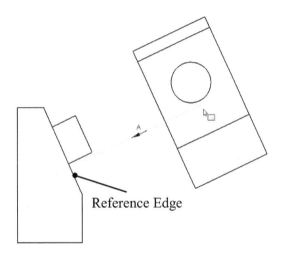

Reference Edge

Fig 11-24 Auxiliary View

The auxiliary view is projected at a right angle from the reference edge and aligned parallel to the reference edge.

You can break alignment by right-clicking on the auxiliary view and choosing Alignment > Break Alignment in the pop-up menu. You can restore the default alignment in the same manner.

 Breaking Alignment

You can break the alignment of an auxiliary view while creating by pressing the Ctrl key.

11.4.3 Section View

By defining a cut line that passes through a specific location in the 3D geometry, you can express a complex shape precisely and effectively. The cut face is hatched. Four cutting line options are available; Vertical, Horizontal, Auxiliary, Aligned. You can create a half section view by pressing the Half Section button.

Fig 11-25 Section View Assist   **Fig 11-26** Half Section View Assist

There are two methods in defining a cutting line and creating a section view.

1. Click the Section View icon and select a passing object. The cutting line is defined, and you can create a section view.
2. Create the cutting line by using the sketch commands. Select all of the sketch curves and click the Section View icon. When you are selecting sketch curves, right-click on a curve and choose Select Chain in the pop-up menu.

The above approaches are valid when you are creating a detail view and a broken-out section view.

If you want to create a stepped section view as shown in Fig 11-28, select the first passing point **Ⓐ**, choose the option **Ⓑ**, and then select the next passing point. You can edit the cutting line by dragging it. You have to rebuild the drawing view after editing the cutting line.

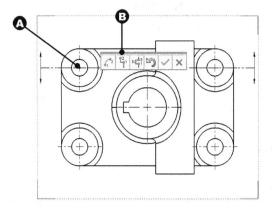

Fig 11-27 Creating Stepped Section View

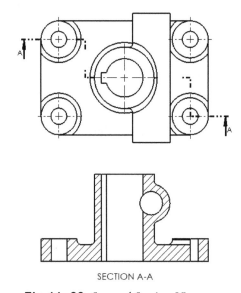

SECTION A-A

Fig 11-28 Stepped Section View

❗ *Removing Tangent Edge*

You can remove tangent edges in a drawing view by right-clicking on the view and choosing Tangent Edges > Tangent Edges Removed in the pop-up menu.

The cutting lines in an aligned section view are neither parallel nor perpendicular. The cutting line **❶-❸** is aligned on the cutting line **❶-❷**. It is called a revolved section view because the cutting line **❶-❸** is revolved about point **❶**.

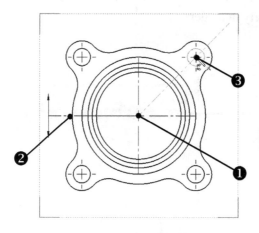

Fig 11-29 Creating Aligned Section View

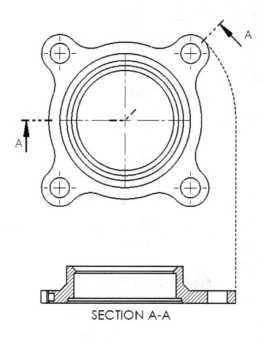

SECTION A-A

Fig 11-30 Aigned Section View

You can create a half section view for a symmetric drawing view as shown in Fig 11-31. You can exclude the Rib features being hatched by choosing them in the design tree. If you want to edit options for a drawing view, select a view and press the Property Manager button. The Section Scope option is available by pressing the More Properties button at the bottom of the property manager.

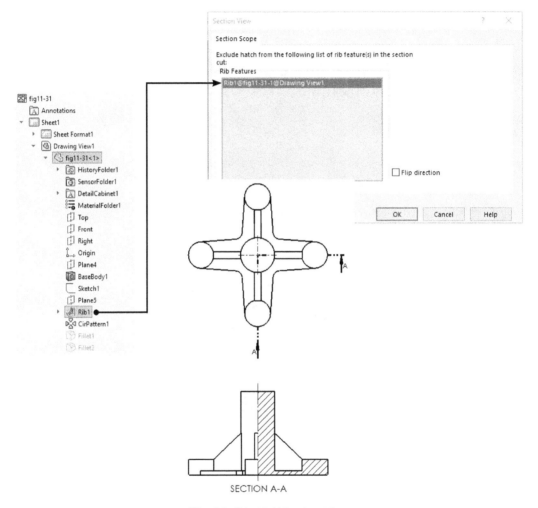

Fig 11-31 Half Section View

11.4.4 Detail View

You can magnify a region of a drawing view to create a detail view by applying a higher scaling ratio. Keep the following process.

1. Create a parent view.
2. Click the Detail View icon.
3. Create a circle to define a region to be magnified.
4. Click a position to locate the detail view.

You can drag the circle to re-define it.

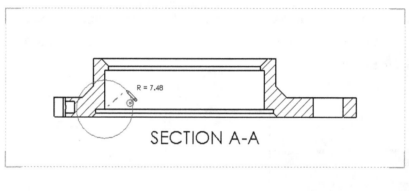

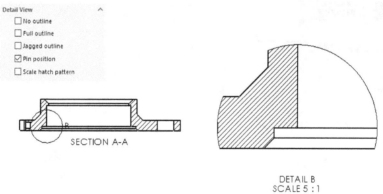

Fig 11-32 Detail View

11.4.5 Broken-Out Section View

A portion of an existing view is cut out at a specified depth. The broken-out region is hatched. When you define the depth, you can select a straight edge, circular edge, or enter a value. Keep the following process.

1. Create parent views to define a broken-out section view.
2. Click the Broken-out Section icon.
3. Create the region to break out.
4. Define the depth to break out.
5. Press OK.

You can create the region to break out by using the sketch commands. Select the closed area and press the Broken-out Section icon. You can use a rectangle or a circle to define the break out region.

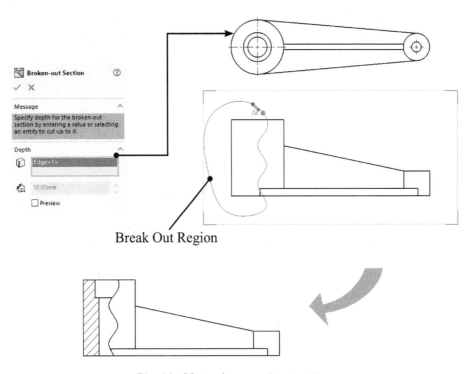

Break Out Region

Fig 11-33 Broken-out Section View

11.4.6 Broken View

You can break out a long uniform section of a part in the middle. Keep the following process.

1. Create a drawing view to create a broken view.
2. Click the Break View icon.
3. Select the drawing view to break.
4. Select the Cutting Direction option.
5. Select a location to define the first break line (Ⓐ in Fig 11-34).
6. Select a location to define the second break line (Ⓑ in Fig 11-34).
7. Press OK.

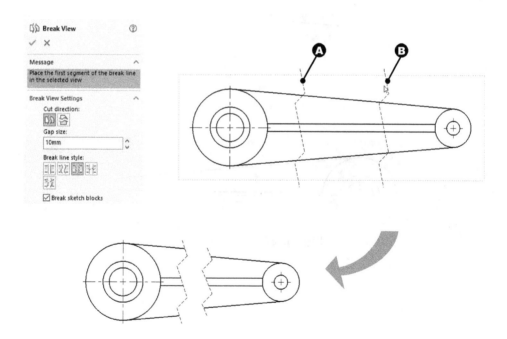

Fig 11-34 Break View

11.4.7 Cropped View

You can remove outside of a closed region from an existing drawing view. Keep the following process.

1. Create a drawing view to create a cropped view.
2. Create a closed profile on the drawing view by using the sketch commands.
3. Press the Crop View icon while the closed profile is selected.

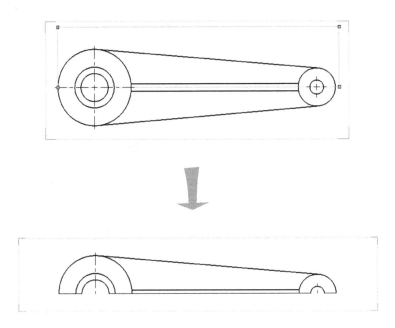

Fig 11-35 Crop View

11.4.8 Removed Section View

You can create a section and remove it from the cut location. This drawing view is used for creating a section for ribs. Keep the following process.

1. Create a drawing view to create a removed section view.
2. Select an edge to define the start of a section (**A** in Fig 11-36).
3. Select the opposite edge to define the end of a section (**B** in Fig 11-36).
4. Place the cutting line (**C** in Fig 11-36).
5. Remove the section out of the geometry and click.
6. Press OK.

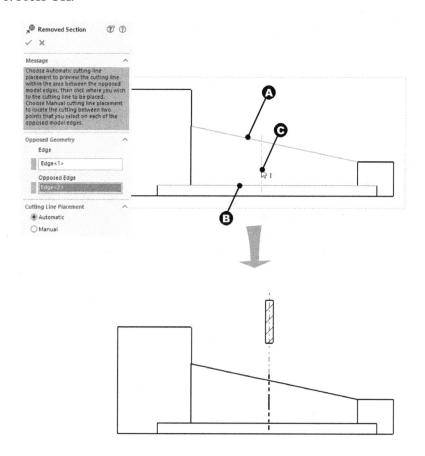

Fig 11-36 Removed Section View

11.5 Layers

You can choose a drafting standard in the document properties dialog box. Fig 11-37 shows the default properties of chamfer dimensions.

You can apply a layer for drafting objects such as dimensions, texts, curves, etc. Note that no layers are applied for the chamfer dimensions.

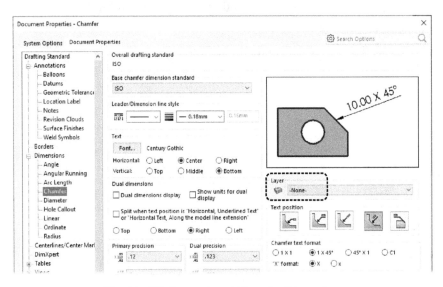

Fig 11-37 Properties of Chamfer Dimensions

You can add the layer toolbar by right-clicking on the command manager. You can check the properties of layers by pressing the Layer Properties button in the Layer toolbar. You can also create new layers in the dialog box. If you choose a layer in the layer dropdown, the layer is assigned to the drafting objects, and the properties defined for the layer are applied to the drafting objects. You can select drafting objects and assign them to another layer.

Fig 11-38 Layer Toolbar

If you press the Layer Properties button in the Layer toolbar, the Layers window is invoked as shown in Fig 11-39. Note that the layer "FORMAT" is created by default. You can define display status, printing, color, style, and thickness for a layer. You can create a new layer by pressing the New button. You can assign a layer for the types of drafting objects in the document properties.

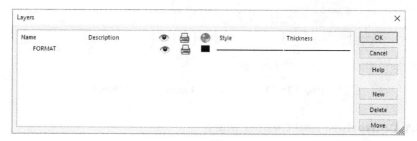

Fig 11-39 Layers Window

The layers "Dimension Lines" and "Center Lines" are created in Fig 11-40. If you have assigned a layer for a drafting object in the document properties, you can apply it by choosing Per Standard in the Layer dropdown when you are creating the drafting object.

If the Line Font and Line Style for a drafting object are specified in the document properties, they take priority over the layers. For example, if you create a centerline by using the Centerline command with a layer specified, the thickness and style for the centerline in the document properties are applied instead of those of the layer.

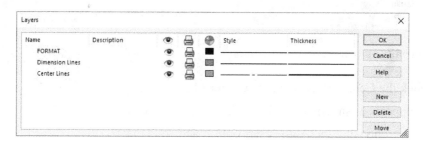

Fig 11-40 Added Layers

11.6 Annotations

You can create dimensions, surface finish symbols, weld symbols, geometric tolerances, centerlines, hatching, notes, etc. by using commands in the Annotation command manager.

Fig 11-41 Annotation Command Manager

11.6.1 Centerline and Center Mark

The center marks of the holes are added automatically, by default, when you create a drawing view. You can alter the options by clicking Options > Document Properties > Detailing > Auto Insert on View Creation.

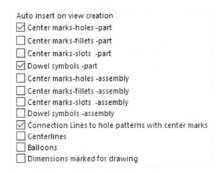

Fig 11-42 Auto Insert on View Creation

If you click the Center Mark icon, the Center Mark property manager appears as shown in Fig 11-43. You can insert center marks by choosing the Auto Insert option and selecting the drawing views.

You can create center mark manually by choosing a type in the Manual Insert Options and selecting the objects. You can insert a circular center mark, as shown in Fig 11-46, by picking three or more circles that are arrayed circularly.

Fig 11-43 Center Mark Property Manager

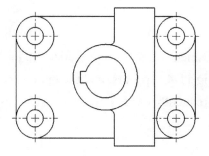

Fig 11-44 Single Center Mark

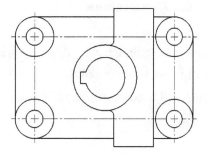

Fig 11-45 Linear Center Mark

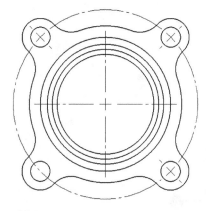

Fig 11-46 Circular Center Mark

By using the Centerline command, you can create centerlines by selecting cylindrical objects(**Ⓐ** in Fig 11-47) or by selecting two lines.

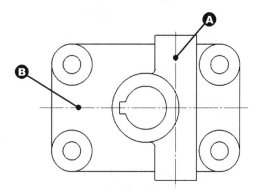

Fig 11-47 Centerline

11.6.2 Dimensions

You can create dimensions by using the Smart Dimension icon. If you click the location for a dimension, a symbol designated by **Ⓐ** in Fig 11-48 appears, and the options shown in Fig 11-49 become available. You can set the frequently used options in the dimensioning option box.

You can set the general options for a dimension in the Dimension property manager as shown in Fig 11-50.

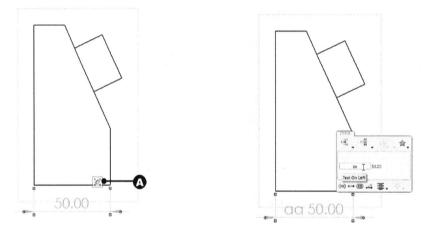

Fig 11-48 Dimensioning

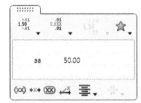

Fig 11-49 Dimensioning Options

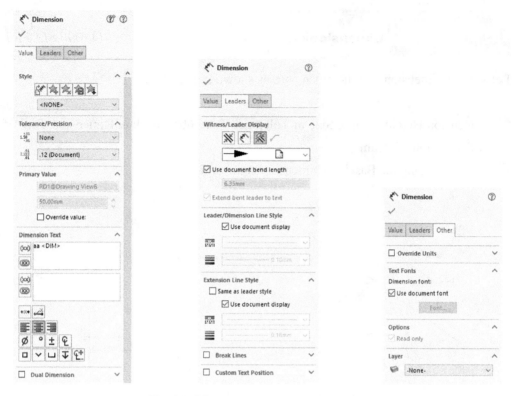

Fig 11-50 Dimension Property Manager

If you uncheck the Use Document Display option in the Leaders tab, you can set the corresponding options manually. If you uncheck the Use Document Font option in the Other tab, you can set the Font options manually. The Tolerance Font Size option is available for dimensions with tolerance.

Fig 11-51 Other Tab for Dimension with Tolerance

Dimensioning   *ch11_003.SLDPRT*

Let's insert dimensions for the given part, as shown in Fig 11-52.

A: Dimension Height 5.5mm, Size of Tolerance Text: 60% of Main Dimension, Size of Other Dimensions: 3.5mm
B: Create by using the Baseline Dimension command.

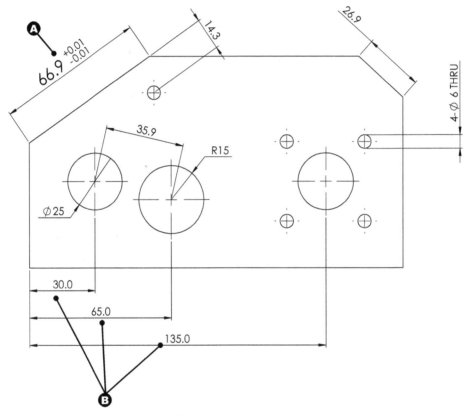

Fig 11-52 Exercise 03

END of Exercise

 **Format Painter**

By using the Format Painter, you can copy appearances of a dimension to apply to another dimensions.

Let's insert dimensions for the given part, as shown in Fig 11-53.

Ⓐ: Create a layer as the name of "Virtual Curve" (Style: Phantom, Color: Black, Thickness: 0.18mm)", and create sketch curves for intersection in the layer.

Ⓑ: Create a radial dimension and apply the Foreshorten option in the Leaders tab.

Ⓒ: Click the Model Items icon. Choose Marked for Drawing, Hole Wizard Profiles and Hole Wizard Locations options in the Dimensions option and select the hole, then alter the style.

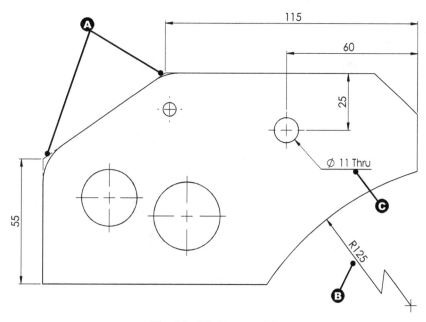

Fig 11-53 Exercise 04

 Alt Key

You drag dimensions precisely by pressing the Alt key.

11.6.3 Note

You can create notes by using the Note command. Fig 11-54 **Ⓐ** shows a text type note, and **Ⓑ** shows a note with leader. You can apply a double leader by selecting the arrow tip and Ctrl + dragging. You can delete a leader by selecting the arrow tip and pressing Delete.

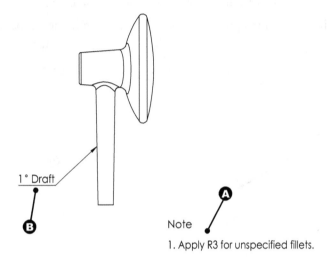

Fig 11-54 Notes

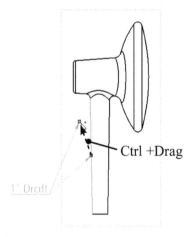

Fig 11-55 Double Leader

Create a drawing for the given part, as shown in Fig 11-56.

1. Make it be the same the figure as possible, except for the frame and title block.
2. Note for the size and scale of the drawing sheet.
3. Apply 4.5mm text height.
4. Do not show the trailing zeros. (Hint: Options > Document Properties > Dimensions)

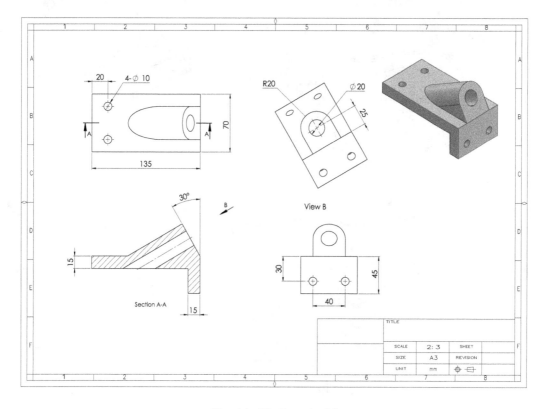

Fig 11-56 Exercise 05

Creating a Drawing *ch11_006.SLDPRT*

Create a drawing for the given part, as shown in Fig 11-57.

1. Make it be the same the figure as possible, except for the frame and title block.
2. Note for the size and scale of the drawing sheet.
3. Apply 4mm text height.

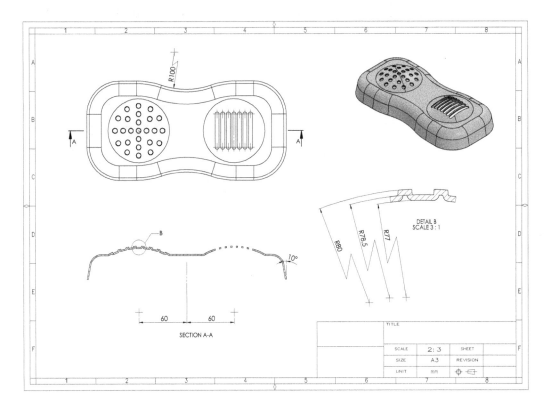

Fig 11-57 Exercise 06

Create a drawing for the given part, as shown in Fig 11-58.

1. Apply 4mm text height.

2. Hide unnecessary edges by using the Hide/Show Edges tool in the Line Format toolbar.

3. Resize the drawing view by using the Crop View command.

4. To create an intersection symbol for fillet, select the two lines, and press the Point icon in the Sketch command manager.

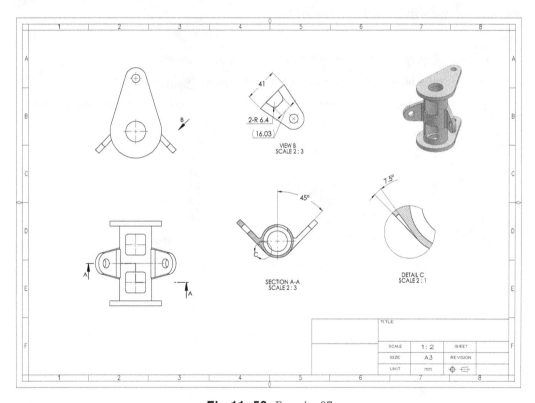

Fig 11-58 Exercise 07

11.7 Assembly Drawing

You can create a drawing for an assembly. The purpose of creating an assembly drawing is to provide the information required for assembling a product. The assembly sequence and path can be illustrated in a disassembled drawing view. Names, quantity, material, etc. of each component of an assembly can be included in the parts list.

To create an assembly drawing, open the assembly file, create a drawing file and insert the drawing views as shown in Fig 11-59 as you have done for the part drawings. You can create a disassembled drawing view, apply balloon annotations and include a parts list. In this chapter, we will learn the following topics.

① Excluding specific components in the assembly drawing view.
② Creating a broken-out section view for an assembly drawing view.
③ Creating a disassembled view and inserting a parts list and balloon annotation.

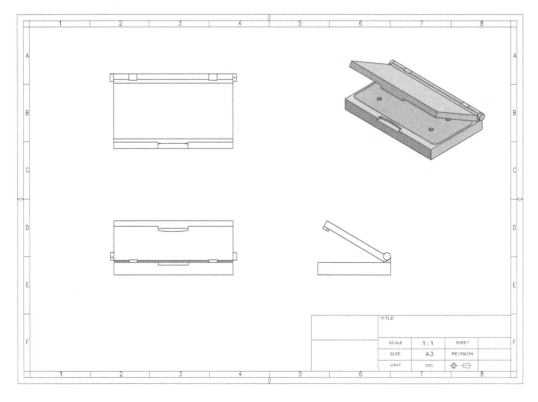

Fig 11-59 Drawing for notebook assy

11.7.1 Excluding Components in a View

Press the More Properties button (❶ in Fig 11-60) at the bottom of the Drawing View property manager. Press the Hide/Show Components tab and select a component by expanding the assembly (❷ in Fig 11-60). If you have already created a drawing view, expand the assembly in a drawing view, right-click on a component and choose Hide/Show > Hide Component in the pop-up menu.

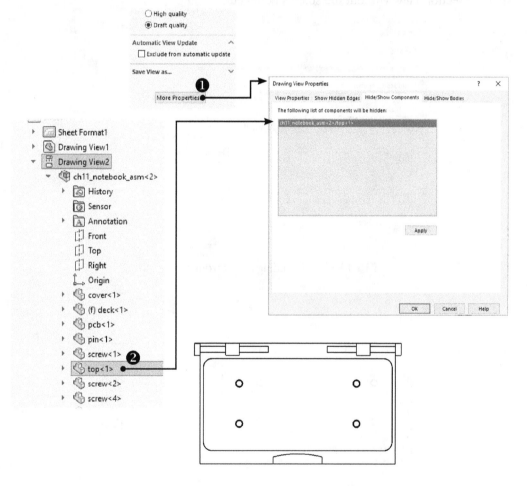

Fig 11-60 Excluding Top Component

11.7.2 Excluding a Component from being Sectioned

When you create a section view for an assembly, you can exclude certain components from being cut. If you define a cutting line and place a section view, the Section View dialog box is invoked as shown in Fig 11-61, and you can specify components to be excluded from the section cut. If you have already created a section view, you can access the dialog box by pressing the More Properties button and pressing the Section Scope tab. Fig 11-62 shows a section view without the screws being cut.

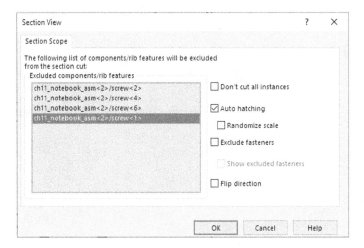

Fig 11-61 Excluding Screw from being Cut

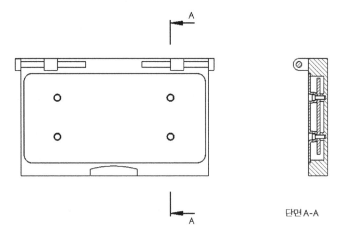

Fig 11-62 Section without Screw being Cut

11.7.3 Broken-out Section View for an Assembly Drawing View

It is hard to describe the assembly state for interior components. In this case, the broken -out section view can be helpful. The procedure is the same as that for the part drawing. Fig 11-64 shows the broken-out section view of the notebook assembly. Keep the following process to create the broken-out section view of an assembly.

1. Create a closed region by using the sketch commands (❶ in Fig 11-63).
2. Press the Broken-out Section icon while the closed cut region is selected.
3. Select the excluded components/rib features and press OK.
4. Select an object to define the cut depth (❹ in Fig 11-63).
5. Press OK in the Broken-out Sections property manager.

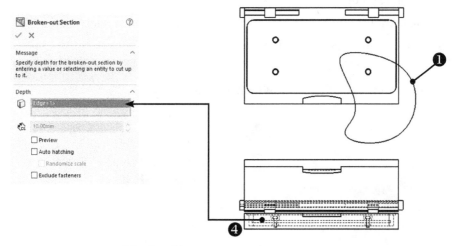

Fig 11-63 Creating Broken-Out Section

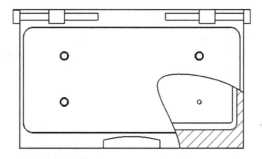

Fig 11-64 Broken-out Section View

11.7.4 Exploded View

The purpose of the exploded drawing view is to illustrate the assembling position of each component. Therefore, the components are not located in the assembled position, but they are moved in a manner to illustrate the assembling relationship effectively.

You can create a parts list automatically for the assembly drawing view, and you can create balloon annotations in the assembly drawing view.

Keep the following process to create an exploded drawing view and parts list.

① Open an assembly file.
② Create an exploded view.
③ Create a drawing view using the exploded configuration created in step ①.
④ Insert bill of material and balloon annotation.

Fig 11-65 shows the exploded view of notebook assembly.

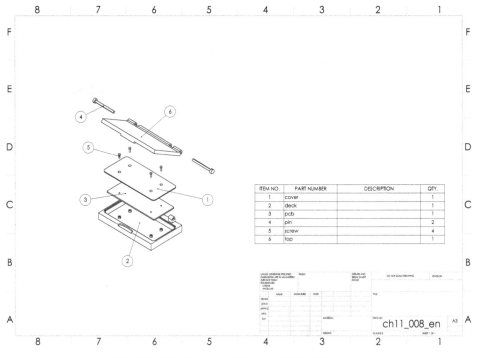

ITEM NO.	PART NUMBER	DESCRIPTION	QTY.
1	cover		1
2	deck		1
3	pcb		1
4	pin		2
5	screw		4
6	top		1

Fig 11-65 Exploded View and Bill of Material

Open the given assembly file (ch11_noteboook_asm) and create an exploded view, parts list, and balloon annotation.

Exploding Assembly

1. Open the given assembly file.
2. Click the Exploded View icon in the Assembly command manager.

Fig 11-67 shows the exploded assembly. The number of steps may differ.

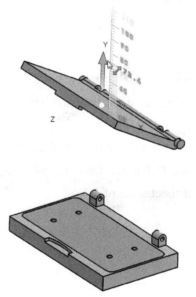

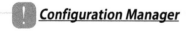
Fig 11-66 Exploding Assembly

! *Configuration Manager*

You can manage the exploded views in the configuration manager.

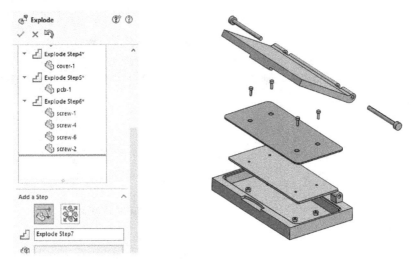

Fig 11-67 Exploded Assembly

Creating Exploded View

1. Choose File > Make Drawing from Assembly in the SOLIDWORKS menu.

2. Choose A3(ANSI) Landscape and press the Next button in the Model View property manager.

3. Drag Isometric Exploded in the View Palette and drop on the sheet. You can choose another exploded view in the Reference Configuration option in the Drawing View command manager. Apply a sheet scale of 2:3.

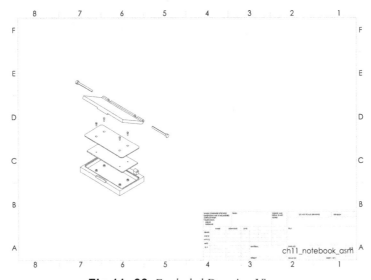

Fig 11-68 Exploded Drawing View

1. Choose Bill of Material under the Table icon group in the Annotation command manager.

2. Select the exploded view.

3. Press OK in the Bill of Material property manager.

4. Pick the location of the table in the sheet.

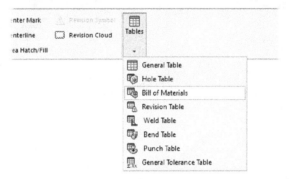

Fig 11-69 Bill of Material Icon

Fig 11-70 Auto Balloon

1. Select the exploded view, and click the Auto Balloon icon in the Annotation command manager.

2. Select a pattern type in the property manager and press OK.

3. Drag the balloon and the location of the arrow tip.

4. Save the drawing file.

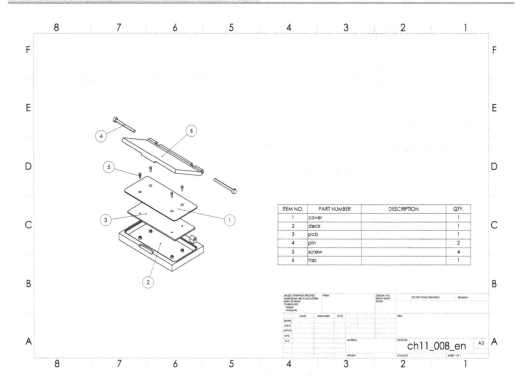

ITEM NO.	PART NUMBER	DESCRIPTION	QTY.
1	cover		1
2	deck		1
3	pcb		1
4	pin		2
5	screw		4
6	top		1

Fig 11-71 Bill of Material and Balloon Annotation

END of Exercise

Index

This page left blank intentionally.

This page left blank intentionally.